CW00971869

boys
are
they really
ALIENS
?

piccadilly press • london

Designed by **wilson design associates**

Phototypeset from author's disk by Piccadilly Press.
Printed and bound by Hartnolls Ltd., Bodmin, Cornwall
for the publishers Piccadilly Press Ltd.,
5 Castle Road, London NW1 8PR

A catalogue record for this book is available from the British Library

ISBN: 1 85340 361 X (hardback)
1 85340 356 3 (trade paperback)

Marina Gask is a young journalist who lives in Herne Hill, South London. She has worked on *Just Seventeen* and is now Features Editor of *Sugar* magazine. This is her first book.

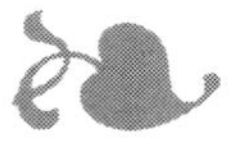

With many thanks to Gill, Tad,
Jacqui, Tony, the Gask family,
everyone at *Sugar* magazine
and all the boys I've
ever been out with.

CONTENTS

Section Four 90-118

DATING

♥♥ INTRODUCTION ♥♥

Judging by the behaviour of some boys, you'd be forgiven for thinking they have more in common with a many-tentacled antennaed green thing than they do with you! Boys can be pretty strange creatures at the best of times. This book tells you all about what they think, what they do, and why the heck they do what they do.

Not *everything* I've said will apply to *every* boy. So please bear this in mind when you're thinking, "Hang on, my mate Simon doesn't behave like that!" This book is about your average boy – a combination of all types of boy.

Section 1

WHAT ARE THEY REALLY LIKE?

A. BOYS ON THEIR OWN

I) HOW THEY THINK THEY SHOULD LOOK

Don't Call Me Mr Vain

Boys like to pretend that they don't give a damn what they look like, that they haven't been near a comb in years and only ever look in the mirror to pull faces. But in reality most boys care *very* much about their appearance and, just like girls, they're terrified that everyone thinks they're "the ugly one" in the crowd.

Boys don't really find it acceptable for other boys to run around primping and preening and fussing with their hair. Consequently, they all tend to feel a bit self-conscious about using cover-up stick on their spots, and you certainly won't catch them moaning in public about having a bad hair day, like most girls would. Boys have to act as if they don't really care about their looks and personal hygiene, as though they just happen to have turned up looking good and not smelling disgusting.

The understated look

The way boys avoid being accused of unmanly vanity is by being understated about their looks and, in some cases, pretending to be slobs. Most of them tend to go for muted colours (dark green, navy, black and grey being the old favourites) and simple, unfussy styles, but always with the *right* trainers and the coolest (or most studiedly unkempt) haircut. That way they can't be accused of girlie preening, but still retain their credibility as someone who looks good sort of accidentally. Think of Damon from Blur. He looks like he's been casually thrown together and never been near a comb, yet he's gorgeous. Well that's what most boys aspire to.

"Girls all really want to go out with musclemen with hairy chests and long hair and suntans. Guys like that really fancy themselves. I think they look right prats."

Warren, 16

"All the girls I know like blokes with flash cars and fancy clothes, smooth types like that guy in Brookside that Katie and Jackie fell out over. He fancies himself something chronic."

Ged, 15

The things that worry boys the most about their looks

Being spotty
Lack of body and facial hair
Being short
Being really tall and lanky
Being puny
Being fat
Greasy hair
Having a big nose or other noticeable feature
Having a protruding Adam's apple
Looking too young

"Looking smart is really important to girls. They'd rather be seen with someone dressed in a flashy suit than scruffy jeans. Neat haircuts and fancy clothes are what count to girls."

Jimmy, 13

"I'm sick of hearing about how gorgeous Keanu Reeves is. He's dead scruffy but he gets away with it because he's naturally good-looking. If I tried to dress like him I'd just get laughed at!"

Frank, 17

II) PUBERTY PROBLEMS

Everything changes

Like girls, boys' hormones start raging when they hit their teenage years, and they find themselves going through some weird changes. Their voices can break almost overnight. One day they're singing soprano, and the next they wake up croaking like a frog with tonsillitis.

Boys greet this sometimes dramatic change of vocal key with mixed feelings. On the one hand, their voice is suddenly out of their control and the object of everyone's amusement. On the other hand, it signals the onset of *manhood,* which is an exciting thing.

Along with their voices breaking, their Adam's apples can start to protrude more, their knees can get knobblier, and their bodies become more muscly and defined. Of course, as you well know, not all boys instantly develop a physique like Howard from Take That – in fact, some look more akin to Mr Bean! – but this is the point where growth spurts occur and general manliness starts to develop.

Of course, this means that any boy who suddenly finds himself a foot taller than the previous week – unlike his mates who're growing at a less alarming rate – or whose Adam's apple sticks out to a very noticeable degree, will be feeling *very* self-conscious during this time, just like girls who find themselves developing noticeably slower or faster than everyone else.

Skin stuff

Strange things happen to boys' faces during puberty.

With all that male hormone – testosterone – racing around, their faces often break out in ugly spots. Girls have this problem too, but for boys acne does tend to be far more severe, and can last for longer. The problem is made far worse by the greasy hair that comes with puberty: as they hang their long fringes over their spots to cover them up, they end up despositing yucky grease on them, which doesn't help them clear up!

Boys don't tend to like doing the sensible thing of going to a doctor or chemist and asking for advice – it's just not done to make a *fuss* about such superficial things. But that doesn't mean that they aren't alarmed at the state of their skin, nor that they don't dread being called "Pizza-Face" by some bright spark in their class.

Some boys get very paranoid if their chins remain hairless while their mates are all having to shave every other day. In fact, some will start shaving long before they actually need to, just like some girls will start wearing bras before they've got anything to support! This is because facial hair is the most obvious sign of manliness in a developing teenage boy, and there's nothing worse than feeling that you're being left behind.

Boys and their bits

If that lot wasn't bad enough, there's far more embarrassing stuff afoot. Whilst they're in the process of maturing sexually, boys can start to get aroused over literally anything – the motion of a bus, the sight of someone they fancy, a washing machine on short spin – I mean, *anything*! This means that they can get tricky-to-hide lumps in their trousers (erections) at the most inopportune moments of the day. Highly embarrassing.

Now this doesn't mean that all boys are rampant sex beasts. No. It's just that during adolescence, their hormones – like yours – go a bit haywire and start to misbehave, causing these untimely erections. Unsurprisingly, most boys are pretty alarmed when this happens to them – suddenly one part of their body seems to have developed a mind and will all of its own, and refuses to be controlled! Well how would *you* feel? Although erections never become an *entirely* controllable thing in a lad's life, thankfully they do tend to calm down a bit when they get to about 16.

During their early teens most boys also start having "wet dreams" – ejaculating during their sleep. This doesn't necessarily mean that they're having naughty dreams; in fact, it's merely their bodies' way of exercising this new function of ejaculation while they're asleep. As you can imagine, this can be a little alarming at first, especially when they have to explain the state of their bedsheets to their mums!

Seriously whiffy

Another unfortunate thing about puberty is the way boys' bodies start to smell. For the first time they suffer from bad breath, sweaty armpits, greasy-smelling hair and whiffy feet – a veritable *pong factory*! Anyone with a teenage brother will know only too well how his socks whiff like an over-ripe cheese and probably yearns for the day when he discovers deodorant as one of life's essentials. The good news is that boys soon realise there's no way any girl is going to go out with them if they don't smell nice.

This means that, once they've discovered girls, boys actually start washing their hair more than once a week, changing their socks daily *and* using deodorant – amazing!

"I started getting a beard when I was 13 and I hated it because everyone was always making jokes about it. Then I realised they were just jealous!"

Tad, 16

"When I was about 12 I just shot up. I'd always been skinny, but suddenly I was tall as well, and really lanky, with a sticking-out Adam's apple. I used to walk with a stoop to be less noticeable. I looked a total geek."

Tony, 16

"The worst thing is watching your mates start shaving and getting really tall, when you still look like a little boy. When I was 15 I looked about 11 – I was small and skinny, with no hair on my body or face. I used to check my face every single day for signs of a beard."

Chris, 18

III) THEIR EMOTIONAL LIFE

Feeling inadequate

Boys, just like girls, dread being inadequate in any way and feeling like an outcast. Boys who think they are small, puny, ugly, etc, will often compensate for their feelings of inadequacy in extreme ways. Often the small boy in your form will also be the class joker, the cheekiest and funniest boy you know, a talent he's probably developed in order to compensate for his short stature.

But sometimes the ways in which boys compensate for their feelings of insecurity aren't so appealing. Some boys will resort to heavily macho behaviour, such as loud swearing, spitting, being crude, telling tasteless jokes, and being really horrible to girls.

A big source of boys' insecurity is the thought of not being fancied. Unlike girls, who may well spend a few hours a day openly swooning over boys they fancy, lads are far less likely to admit to fancying someone who might not fancy them back. It's more than their pride can take!

The fear of not being fancied affects boys just as much as girls. The difference is in how they deal with it. Whereas girls might blame themselves for not being attractive enough and go to great lengths to make themselves more appealing, boys are more likely to blame the girls that don't fancy them and give them a hard time for it. Charming, eh?

Being soft

Boys do not like to talk about their feelings. So while they'll happily natter on about football, bogies, girls, Sega, trainers, Oasis, what they saw on T.V. last night, etc, they'd rather have their teeth pulled out *one by one* than admit to having feelings.

Well, believe it or not, they have plenty of them. They may not cry at soppy films like *Ghost* (and think it's hilarious to snigger at you when *you* do), but that doesn't mean that they aren't as squishy as a jellyfish under all that bravado.

In most boys' eyes, acknowledging emotions is like saying "I'm a big girlie wet". In fact, to some boys, it's just one step away from being gay! And few teenage boys are mature enough to realise that there is nothing wrong with being gay.

Lads show their feelings differently and over different things. It's okay for a boy to weep openly when he scores the winning goal in his school match, whereas he'll spend hours on end in the company of his mates without once mentioning the fact that he's going through some big emotional ordeal, like the divorce of his parents. And likewise, for some boys (most, actually) it's definitely *not* the done thing to tell a girlfriend how he feels about her. So cringingly embarrassed would he be if forced to do this that he'd be more likely to crack some joke and change the subject. A boy needs to feel *v-e-r-y* secure with his girlfriend and equally sure of his own emotions before he'll discuss them with her.

♥ ♥ B. BOYS WITH THEIR MATES ♥ ♥

I) THE INFLUENCE OF THEIR MATES

The group mentality

Boys care very much about looking good in their mates' eyes. Normal, sane, even *pleasant* as they can be on their own (sometimes), in front of their mates, lads have a nasty habit of turning into the local equivalent of *Beavis and Butthead*.

Watch your favourite boy in the company of his pals. Could this swearing, burping, wise-cracking, leering idiot really be the sweet young chap who, when it's just the two of you, helps you with your history homework and calls you Choochy-Face? Well yes, unfortunately it could. You see, the need to be accepted as "one of the lads" and avoid group ridicule is so huge that your boy undergoes a radical personality transplant in the presence of his gang in order to fit in with whatever the gang thinks is cool. It's more than just peer pressure, it's *gang pressure*.

Boys always want to *impress* their friends (and will always hang out with people who're hard to be impressed, otherwise it'd gain them nothing at all). This could involve anything from wowing their mates on the Nintendo to projectile spitting.

Pulling power

That's not to say that they'll have no truck with the female sex – *oooh* no. One way for a boy to impress his mates is by being seen with the Girls To Be Seen With (GTBSW). Being fancied and flirted with by a few GTBSWs is the ultimate macho status symbol, *especially* if the guy in question appears to do it effortlessly. Boys will relish the attention of "fanciable" girls just because it makes them look good rather than because they actually fancy them.

In order to avoid appearing too much of a wuss, a boy will steer well clear of any cutesy hand-holding behaviour, keeping the poor girl at arm's length so it looks like *he's* in control. Hence the well-known girls' refrain: "He's really nice to me when we're on our own, but ignores me and acts like a jerk when his mates are there."

Fear of rejection

No one likes being rejected, but fear of merciless teasing by their mates means that boys find a public humiliation or rejection *unbearable* – particularly by a *girl*. Now you may well spend a fair amount of time asking yourself, "How come that sweet guy I keep meeting at the sports centre/youth club/McDonalds, who always chats to me loads, gets plenty of encouragement from me and can't keep his eyes off me *never asks me out*?!" Well it's a pretty safe bet that the one and only reason is because he's terrified that you'll say no. This would not only wound his fragile ego, but it would also make him look an utter fool in front of his mates if they got wind of it.

The same goes for any form of humiliation. If, for example, you were to go out with one boy, but were seen flirting with another, the hurt he may feel would be doubled by the thought of how it makes him look in the eyes of the world, ie, *inadequate*.

II) COMPETITIVENESS

Playing To Win

It probably hasn't escaped your notice that boys are a mighty competitive bunch. They hate to lose at *anything*. You only have to play Trivial Pursuit, table tennis or even Hungry Hippos with a boy if you want proof. They'll make up new rules, refuse to play, cheat, try to con you, go into a strop, *whatever*, in order to win, and when they do win (usually because somebody's *let* them, just for the sake of the peace), they have to *show off* and make a great big noise about it. How pathetic.

Unfortunately this obsession with winning carries over into every game they play, whether it's football or farting competitions, and this brings out some of the downright childish behaviour that you're doubtless aware of.

One-Upmanship A major part of boysieness is being better than everyone else at something and bragging about it. And the worst kind of one-upmanship boys indulge in is the kind that involves girls. If it involves how many hearts a guy can break, or worse, how far he's gone with a particular girl, then it can have some pretty unpleasant consequences, especially if you happen to be the girl in question. It's a sad fact, but many boys, especially the really insecure ones, will use girls as *trophies* in their silly game of one-upmanship, and this is what so often causes boys to do hurtful things. For instance, you might just have an innocent smooch with a boy at a party, but to make himself look big, he goes and exaggerates the facts to his mates to make out that you did far more together than is strictly true, just like Danny does in the musical *Grease*. Or a guy might make out he really fancies you and ask you out, just so he can tell his mates he's gone on another date and "scored" once again.

III) HOW THEY COMMUNICATE WITH EACH OTHER

What boys talk about Lads spend their time talking about *safe* subjects (ie, not emotional ones) that they all know something about – like sport, for example. They can dissect every move in a 90-minute football match quite happily and never once get bored. They'll run through a *Vic and Bob* sketch, doing all the voices and actions and laughing uproariously, and then they'll run through the whole thing again. They'll describe a motorbike they've just seen in glowing I'm-gonna-get-one-soon admiration. They'll brag about anything they can think of, with much exaggeration of the facts. They'll gossip about who fancies who and who got off with who. And they'll take the mick out of each other, mercilessly and endlessly. Beyond that it's all showing off while simultaneously putting each other down. And that's about it!

What they don't talk about

So conscious are boys of being accepted by their group and sticking to their role within it – be it as the leader, the joker, the butt of every joke, whatever – that they'll do as little as possible to make their mates suspect them of unmasculine behaviour. This means that certain subjects are avoided altogether and on a permanent basis. Ever noticed how a group of lads can spend all their spare time together for weeks on end, completely unaware that one of them has recently had his heart broken? That's because, as we already know, lads just don't discuss their emotions. Hence boys keep their cards close to their chests and act as if problems, fears and upsets just do not exist.

As you can guess, the concept of the New Man makes most lads chuckle heartily – the very thought of someone who carries his girlfriend's shopping home, buys her tampons and openly cries when he discusses his emotions seems utterly ridiculous to them.

In some cases, a lad might feel at ease discussing feelings with his closest male buddy, but only when things are really bad and only in the strictest confidence. As lads get older and stop feeling so *paranoid* about the unmanliness of admitting to having feelings, they get more used to opening up and being honest – although, tragically, in some cases this never happens.

♥ C. LITTLE THINGS YOU SHOULD KNOW ♥

I) WHAT BOYS FIND FUNNY

✔ Reciting Harry Enfield sketches endlessly
✔ Pinging your bra-straps
✔ Each other
✔ Gobbing out of the car window to see how many people they can hit
✔ Inflicting physical pain on each other in the name of male bonding
✔ Attempting to light their own farts
✔ Making jokes of a very personal nature
✔ Having burping contests
✔ Saying "Uh-uh-uh-uh, that *thuckth*" like *Beavis and Butthead*
✔ Making water balloons with condoms
✔ Sniggering at you when you blub during the sad bit in a film
✔ Making "witty" comments about the "time of the month" if you happen to be looking a bit grumpy
✔ Asking you how many Kleenex it took to make your bust so big
✔ Picking on one of your (often imaginary) physical features and turning it into an unpleasant nickname, eg "Big-Bum", "Titsy", "Zit-Face", etc
✔ Saying "I don't do the washing-up – that's a *gurrrl's* job" just to see how wound up you get!
✔ Showing you the contents of their vile, grubby hanky after they've just blown their nose
✔ Swearing every five seconds

✔ Drawing moustache, glasses, pustules and crude speech bubbles all over your fave pic of Keanu Reeves
✔ Making jokes about each other being gay
✔ Eating with their mouths wide open, and forcing you to admire the contents
✔ Getting drunk and falling over

II) INTERESTING MALE FORMS OF EXPRESSION

✌ Burping
✌ Insulting
✌ Silence (when they don't know the answer)
✌ Teasing you when they fancy you
✌ Hitting you when they fancy you
✌ Constantly repeating catchphrases (like "Schwing" when they see a good-looking girl)
✌ Using "In" words that only they understand
✌ Grunting
✌ Sniggering

III) WORDS THAT TERRIFY BOYS

✘ "Love"
✘ "Commitment"
✘ "Relationship"
✘ "Chucked"
✘ "Boyfriend"
✘ "Communicate"
✘ "Gay"
✘ "Wrong"
✘ "Sorry"
✘ "Phone"

IV) FACTS ABOUT BOYS

- ☞ They mature more slowly than girls.
- ☞ They DO bitch and gossip.
- ☞ They can't meet a girl without asking themselves "Do I fancy her?"
- ☞ They tend to operate in packs.
- ☞ They're much nicer on their own.
- ☞ They don't think about sex and girls all the time.
- ☞ Their feet pong more than girls' do.
- ☞ They behave like idiots when their mates are around.
- ☞ They hate being pursued relentlessly.
- ☞ They're pretty unobservant (eg, new hairdos).
- ☞ Their hearts can be broken.
- ☞ They spend most of their time mercilessly taking the mick out of each other.
- ☞ They don't only want to date supermodels and sex kittens.
- ☞ They aren't totally unfeeling and self-assured.
- ☞ They're genuinely mystified by the female sex.
- ☞ They're insecure about their looks.
- ☞ They aren't "all the same".
- ☞ They aren't all bastards.

V) 25 THINGS *(SOME)* BOYS GET WRONG ABOUT GIRLS

1. That girls have made up their own secret rules about dating.

2. That girls only ever talk about boys and snogging.

3. That girls could only possibly like football because they fancy the players.

4. That girls spend hours on end discussing the merits of different tampons.

5. That all girls really want from life is a boyfriend.

6. That all girls' bad moods are caused by PMT.

7. That girls are weaklings and scaredycats who cry if a dog growls at them.

8. That pretty girls want to be hassled.

9. That less pretty girls are there to be teased.

10. That girls gossip constantly.

11. That girls want to turn boys into hand-holding sissies.

12. That girls can't catch a ball to save their lives.

13. That girls don't fart.

14. That girls wash their hair every five minutes.

15. That girls were born to nag.

16. That the absolute best way to chat girls up is to tease them.

17. That girls who don't date or openly fancy boys must be lesbians.

18. That all girls are ridiculously vain.

19. That a girl who's good at Maths can't be normal.

20. That most girls are happy to hang around in McDonald's when they're on a "date".

21. That girls kiss all their hunk pics on their bedroom walls each and every night.

22. That girls are only interested in snowboarding because cute boys are.

23. That if you kiss a girl she'll start planning the wedding.

24. That no girl is capable of being friends with a boy without fancying him.

25. That all girls just adore babies.

PLEASE READ THIS – THIS IS V. IMPORTANT!

↓ ↓ ↓ ↓

VI) WHAT BOYS HAVE IN COMMON WITH GIRLS

- They have feelings.
- They're as scared of you as you are of them.
- They like snogging.
- They're insecure.
- They gossip.
- They worry that no one fancies them.
- They're vain.
- They're bitchy.
- They're easily hurt.
- They're insecure about their looks.

GIRLS BOYS GIRLS BOYS GIRLS BOYS

SOME THINGS BOYS TALK ABOUT

Music
Girls and snogging
Films
Who did what with whom
What they did at the weekend
What's happening in the soaps
Who fancies who
How gorgeous such-and-such is
How much they hate their geography teacher
What's going on next weekend
What a jerk such-and-such is

SOME THINGS GIRLS TALK ABOUT

Music
Boys and snogging
Films
Who did what with whom
What they did at the weekend
What's happening in the soaps
Who fancies who
How gorgeous such-and-such is
How much they hate their geography teacher
What's going on next weekend
What a jerk such-and-such is

GIRLS GIRLS BOYS BOYS

MY SPOT PROBLEM

I have really bad spots. Sometimes they're so bad, it looks like I've got bubonic plague! I dread going to school when they're very bad, and get embarrassed if I have to speak to a girl because she's bound to be disgusted by them. What can I do?"

Simon, 14

Dear Simon,

Spots can be very distressing during puberty, which is a time when you feel sensitive enough about the changes happening to your body as it is! When spots are really bad, as you've found out, it can sometimes feel like they control you rather than you controlling them; but this needn't be the case. Go and see your doctor or chemist and ask for a course of treatment to get rid of your acne. Meanwhile, try and cut out anything in your diet that could be making the condition worse, such as processed food, fat and excess sugar. It's also essential that you keep your skin as clean as possible, by using medicated facial cleansers regularly and frequently. Then once you've done all you can to limit the problem, try and forget about it. Easier said than done, I know, but girls won't be nearly as conscious of your spots as you are – they'll be too busy worrying about their own to notice.

I'M ALWAYS FIGHTING

I started going out with this really nice girl about three weeks ago. The only problem is, she hates me fighting. We had a massive row the other day when I caught this boy chatting her up and nearly beat him up. She says she'll finish with me if I don't stop, but I'm not sure I can.

Gary, 14

Dear Gary,
There are many reasons why boys fight. It could be that you've been brought up that way – to use anger and violence to get what you want. Or maybe you're having problems at home and you're using scrapping as a means to vent your frustration. Or maybe you're insecure and you cover up for it by playing the big macho man. Whatever the reason, you have to stop fighting, if not for your girlfriend, for yourself. Apart from the obvious dangers of getting seriously hurt, you could end up in trouble with the police, and then who knows where it could end. If you find that you're full of aggression, get involved in a sport so you can take it out on an energetic activity. It's far more productive to pound out your aggression on a football pitch than on someone's face, and it causes considerably less damage. If you're still feeling frustrated and angry, talk it through with your girlfriend or your parents and try to get to the root of the problem. And remember: violence doesn't solve any problems, it only creates new ones.

I CALLED HER A SLAG

I got off with this girl at a party, and went up to a bedroom with her. We didn't actually have sex, we just touched each other, but I went and told everyone that we had sex. Now everyone at school is calling her a slag, and I wish I'd never said it. What can I do?

Jonathan, 15

Dear Jonathan,

You've put yourself in a very difficult position. If you carry on the lie, you'll have it on your conscience forever. If you admit it was a lie, you'll lose face in front of everyone. Now put yourself in this girl's shoes. Everyone's calling her names because of your bragging, and she's feeling humiliated and isolated. That's no good at all is it? Whatever the cost to yourself you *must* apologise to this girl and rectify the situation. Write her a letter or tell her to her face, but let her know that you regret what you did. Let everyone else know it was a lie. Then put it all behind you and try to forget about it. Ultimately people have a lot more respect for honesty than they do for bragging, so you'll know you took the right course of action in the end.

Section 2

HOW THEY VIEW YOU

A. WHAT BOYS LOOK FOR IN GIRLS

I) LOOKS

Hey, Good-Lookin' Most boys are incapable of discussing a girl without talking about the way she looks. For some boys it's *all* they can talk about! So in awe are they of the *female mystique* that they find it easier to deal with girls as a concept if they talk about them purely in terms of boobs and bums.

But, more than likely, the main reason for referring to girls purely in terms of how much they fancy them – or don't is that boring old male one-upmanship again. It's a way of showing off, of saying, "I know a good-looking bird when I see one," of being really blokish and making their mates laugh by making crude or unflattering comments.

In reality, although they may be outwardly impressed with super-glam girls, most of them aren't half as bothered about how a girl looks as they make out. But for the benefit of their mates, it's pretty much all they're interested in.

How boys like girls to look

Some girls go to an awful lot of trouble to make themselves look how they think boys want them to look – high heels, slinky dresses, starvation diets, wonderbras and heaps of make-up – just to make all the boys slaver and drool and queue up to ask them out. Pamela Anderson and Kim Basinger have made their fortune from looking saucy, so why shouldn't it work for you?

Well, believe it or not, this is all *completely unnecessary*. Sure, the lads you know may go "Cor!" and turn into whimpering puppies every time Cindy Crawford shimmies across another catwalk, but the fact is, if *you* were to turn up dolled up like Cindy, real boys would be utterly *terrified* of you. Ask virtually any boy what he thinks about make-up, and he'll say, "I like girls to look natural."

The same goes for having a supermodel figure. I mean, if you happen to have one naturally, then few lads are going to complain, but if you happen to be a bit more curvy, then plenty of lads will fancy you too. At the end of the day, any boy worth his salt will like you for *who you are*, not the width of your waist or the size of your bust.

Girls who girls think boys fancy

Glamorous, show-offy types who are all just too intimidating for words...

Madonna

Anna Nicole Smith

Sharon Stone

Helena Christensen

Cindy Crawford

Claudia Schiffer

Pamela Anderson

Linda Evangelista

Christy Turlington

Julia Roberts

Girls who boys really fancy

Less over the top types who they'd really feel more at home with...

Janet Jackson

Kylie Minogue

Uma Thurman

Michelle Pfeiffer

Louise Nurding,
formerly from Eternal

II) PERSONALITY

Boys are often terrified of girls who are really extrovert and confident. They may well admire them from afar – just the same way that they admire Claudia Schiffer at a great distance – but deep down they *quake* at the very thought of them. *How could I impress a girl like that? What if she showed me up?* These are the fears that torment them when faced with an overly sassy female. When it comes to girls they actually feel comfortable with – and therefore want to date – they'd much rather be with someone a bit more down-to-earth and unassuming. That way they don't feel like they have to compete with you, which means that they can *relax* and feel at ease.

This isn't to say that, if you're a bit of an extrovert, you should keep quiet about it in order to be more attractive to boys! Just bear in mind the fact that lads are easily intimidated, and feel out of their depth if your personality's *too* overpowering.

Boys like girls who...

- ✔ they can talk to and have a laugh with
- ✔ make them feel good about themselves
- ✔ don't intimidate them
- ✔ they can trust
- ✔ make them look good in front of their mates
- ✔ don't act "superior" with them
- ✔ aren't vain or bitchy
- ✔ don't get clingy and demanding
- ✔ are independent and have a mind of their own
- ✔ don't wear so much make-up that they don't want to kiss you for fear of getting covered in it

III) STYLE

When it comes to how you dress, the trick is to be comfortable with how you look and to make the most of your features. Lads are always impressed by girls who exude *calm self-confidence*. Dressing in clothes and colours that really suit you and feeling totally at ease with your image will make you infinitely more attractive to the opposite sex than any amount of low-cut lycra and glossy lipstick.

Of course, this calm self-confidence in the way you look is quite hard to come by, but experimenting with your clothes and consulting your closest friends to figure out what suits you best (and avoiding anything remotely unflattering like the plague) will definitely help. Also, believe it or not, pretending to be confident actually helps you to *become* confident!

Lads tend to have a lot of respect for girls who take care of themselves and look after their appearance. Clean, well-cut hair, a little carefully applied make-up and clothes that suit you will show everyone that you take pride in yourself, which any truly *dateable* boy will find infinitely more appealing than in-yer-face sexy clothes and glossy red lips. Good news!

B. WHAT FASCINATES BOYS ABOUT GIRLS

I) YOU AND YOUR FRIENDS

Why do girls all get changed together and spend so long doing it? Why do all girls go to the loo together? Why do they analyse everything? How come they seem to talk about everything with each other, from periods to parents to boys?

Boys are fascinated by female friendships and the strange,

mysterious bond that most girls seem to share with their pals. They find it weird that a girl will spend hours on the phone with her closest chum, even though she's been with her all day at school. They can't quite understand how girls can be so in touch with their emotions all the time and feel close enough to each other to discuss them in great detail – *without* feeling vulnerable afterwards.

These things all make up the *Mysterious World of the Female* to your average lad, who, while he finds it all a bit ridiculous, deep down can't help but feel a bit jealous of girls' closeness. Because while girls are being close, they're dealing with all their feelings and problems, sharing their experience and worldly wisdom with each other, and getting some support, which is something boys find very hard to do.

II) PERIODS, ETC

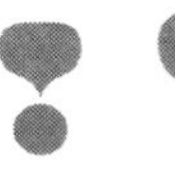

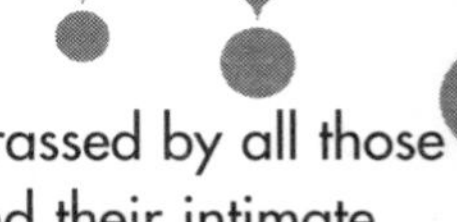

Girls' "thingies"

Boys are mortally embarrassed by all those things that relate to girls and their intimate parts. Mention periods, tampons, bras, PMT, etc, to your average boy and he'll curl up and die on the spot. Oh, yes, there are plenty out there who think it's hilarious to crack jokes about these very things, pinging your bra strap, chucking your tampons round the classroom, etc, but the very reason they do this is because these intimate female things *baffle* them.

But make no mistake, boys *are* curious about all this girls' stuff. Once they get past the embarrassment, they find the workings of the menstrual cycle and the dynamics of the underwired bra quite fascinating! The very same boy who used to chuck your tampons about in class will be full of sympathy and questions the day his girlfriend complains of menstrual cramps. *"Where does it hurt? How does it feel? What can I do to help?"* he'll query, with an awestruck and bemused look on his face.

There are very few boys who *genuinely* think that periods are a disgusting thing, although many will talk as though they are in front of their mates. Of course, if a boy had to suffer the equivalent of a period pain for just five minutes, he'd check himself into the nearest hospital without a moment's delay! Often, the only way that many boys can deal with their fear and cringingness over girls' stuff is to a) crack jokes about it, and b) try to pretend these things just don't exist.

III) YOUR INTERESTS

Girlie stuff

Some boys have pretty weird ideas about what girls like to do with their spare time. They think that girls spend every waking moment dreaming and gossiping about who they fancy – that is, when they're not knitting, making cushion covers or crocheting a hammock for their hamster's cage! This is, of course, a bit clichéd. It also means that boys get a terrible shock when they discover that most girls know how to play computer games or wire a plug unaided.

Because the two sexes are pretty uninterested in each other until adolescence, lads think it a natural progression for girls who used to plait their dollies' hair to spend their lives blow-drying their own now; just in the same way that girls think that boys who used to love rolling around in the sandpit are now interested in nothing but sex and football.

Of course, while boys are pretty fascinated by things girls are interested in, like make-up and clothes and gossiping, they don't like it so much when girls' interests happen to coincide with *their* interests. So if you happen to be a dab-hand with a pool cue or a nifty forward on the footie field, you might find that you only grudgingly earn their respect!

♥ C. WHAT BOYS DISLIKE IN GIRLS ♥

I) MOODINESS

Boys really hate moodiness in girls. As far as they can see, some girls suffer from incomprehensible mood swings and bad tempers for no good reason. Boys don't realise that they can be mighty frustrating beasts. Being late, ignoring you, taking the mick a little *too* much when their mates are there andnot paying you enough romantic attention, are each in themselves sufficient to make some girls lose patience and get fed up. Some particularly unpleasant boys are so unwilling to accept any responsibility for your mood that they'll make jokes about the time of the month and try to blame your grumpiness entirely on your menstrual cycle! Needless to say, such boys are beneath contempt.

II) GOSSIPING AND GIGGLING

Boys hate girls who are very loud and silly with each other: the way some girls like to scream and hug when they meet up after a mere 24 hours apart, for example; how some like to gossip and giggle, endlessly and *in public*, about boys – who-fancies-who, who-looked-at-me-today, etc. And how some girls idolise, scream and generally get over-excited at the likes of Take That and Ryan Giggs.

III) BEING TOO SERIOUS

Getting tied down Most boys are convinced that all girls want is to lure a poor, unsuspecting chap into a scary, serious relationship and keep hold of him *for life*, never letting him see daylight, his friends or the footie ever again. This is what they refer to as "getting tied down," and they consider it a fate worse than death. The stupid thing is, the girl might be just as casual, carefree and out-for-a-laugh as the boy, but that's not going to stop him from thinking that she, like the rest of her sex, is evil, *conniving* and just out to trap him.

Boys also often feel that girls are way too keen to *get serious*, and to go from an easy-going, having-a-laugh type romance, to exchanging rings and meeting the parents in no time at all. And this, understandably, makes them very nervous indeed. It's a major source of paranoia with boys which causes them to start behaving like a *trapped animal* if you so much as suggest that you go record shopping together on Saturday!

The main tip is not to expect too much too soon, keep things nice and easy-going, don't make big emotional demands and expect major commitment after just two weeks of seeing each other.

If, however, as things progress between you, you're still not getting enough evidence of commitment from the lad in question, that's when you need to start the "I want to talk about *us*" conversation. And not before.

Baby, this is serious

Boys hate girls who take things too seriously. Girls, they think, are obsessed with analysing every small detail of any emotional situation – particularly, of course, friendships and romances.

While you may have the *emotional capacity* to deal with the finer details of relationships, most boys have a long way to go in that department. So help them out a bit and don't make mountains out of molehills; save your showdowns for major crimes!

From the heart

Another thing that can leave lads *speechless* with terror is the female capacity to talk about emotions. Whereas a lot of girls resent the fact that boys hate to do this more than visiting their Great-aunt Maude, lads often wish that girls wouldn't do it at all! But it's this female ability to open up, to be frank and honest about all matters emotional that often holds relationships together and keeps things running *smoothly*. If it were left to the lads, nothing would ever get said and no one would ever have a clue how anyone feels.

As we know, for most males, discussing feelings is *very* hard. If you ask them directly about their feelings they'll probably blurt out any old nonsense and change the subject as quickly as possible.

However, boys *do* feel things, just like girls, even if they're not very good at expressing these feelings. The best thing girls can do is to try to help them, by gently coaxing their thoughts out of them. Saying to a boy, "I feel like this about you – don't you want to talk about it?" is better than saying, "What do you feel for me?"

IV) TEASING AND WINDING THEM UP

She's a wind-up

Girls who flash boys *come hither* smiles and give them reason to hope that there might be a romance in the offing when really they're just doing it for fun, are loathed by boys. Fun! Not very funny to play with someone else's emotions, as you well know.

It may seem like a bit of a laugh to test all the lads you know as to how much they fancy you, by flirting a bit with them just to see if it has the desired effect of getting you some attention, but it is seriously *not fair*. So, while a bit of light-hearted flirting won't do anyone any harm, giving a lad some serious encouragement, then telling him to get lost when it comes to the crunch, is seriously *not on*.

V) GOOEY AND LOVEY-DOVEY

Honey-Bunny WUVS Poobum

Lovey-dovey girlfriends are your average boy's biggest nightmare. While your boyfriend may be more than happy to indulge in cutesy hand-holding-type stuff when it's just the two of you, he'll find it deeply cringe-inducing to do it when anyone else – particularly those mates of his – is around. It takes a well-sorted nineties, New Man (does anyone actually *know* any?) to let his girlfriend call him by his pet name in front of his mates, and the same goes for any other kissy-wissy, lovey-dovey stuff. Any girls prone to doing this, be warned: he's more likely to disown you on the spot than call you Snugglebottom (or whatever your pet name is) back.

The same goes for cutesy love notes. While that boy who always catches your eye in History may think you're truly gorgeous, he'd be *mortified* if, say, you passed a note to him saying, "Hi, Cutey-Pie..." in full view of everyone else. For one thing, most boys hate being told they're cute. Fanciable, gorgeous, nice, hunky, scrummy, whatever, but *not* cute. But worse, his or your mates are *bound* to get their hands on that note (these things are just inevitable), and tease the living daylights out of you both – especially him.

And if you happen to be going out with this boy, avoid the slushy stuff in public if you don't want to make the pair of you a laughing stock and make everyone else feel a bit sick to boot. Other people's slushiness is always a bit revolting to witness.

VI) TOO PRETTY, TOO CONFIDENT, TOO SHARP

Miss Sassy There's one breed of female that most of your typical boys find particularly terrifying. This is the kind that's forthright and confident and can hold her own; the loud and proud girls who have Drew Barrymore, Madonna and Tank Girl as their role models. You see, lads like to think that they have the monopoly of assertive behaviour as, traditionally, it's been very much *their thing*.

Many lads will claim, "I like a girl who speaks her mind," or, "I can't stand girls who let themselves get walked all over," but when they feel that girls are in competition with *them*, they're not quite so rapturous about it!

Getting the better of them

Boys fear meeting their female match. As we know, boys hate to be beaten at anything, especially by girls, so they don't tend to welcome a girl with open arms if she happens to be better than them at anything, however much they may secretly admire her.

If a lad's a skateboarder, you would imagine that his ultimate dream girlfriend would be a female skateboarder, wouldn't you? Well not if she happens to be as good – or worse, *better* – than him at it! That's when he feels that his masculinity's being challenged, so his immediate reaction is to be *scornful* of such a girl. Pathetic, eh?

The same goes for a lad who's a bit of a lady-killer. If he's used to having his pick of the girls and to breaking hearts willy-nilly throughout the neighbourhood, he'll be filled with mortal fear the day he meets a girl who happens to do the same with lads.

Miss Manipulative

Certain male members of society don't understand females at all, and so distrust them and think they're out to make them look stupid. Admittedly, certain women – Madonna, to name but one – have made it virtually their life's work to use their feminine wiles to get their own way with blokes, leaving a trail of destruction and broken hearts in their wake. But do you all seriously intend to behave like this? Well hopefully not.

Witness the reaction of a lad when you tell him that you got your mate to suss him out, put in a good word for you and generally match-make the two of you together. Suddenly it's, "I don't *believe* this! I've been framed! It's a set-up! You women, you're so scheming, evil, conniving..." etc.

The same goes for emotional manipulation. If you're in the habit of sulking, turning on the waterworks or – worst of all – threatening to finish with your boy in order to get your own way, then you're going to make a lot of lads very miserable in your lifetime. This sort of thing is seriously *underhand*, and while you may feel that you're forced to resort to such tactics just to get a reaction, it's far better in the long run to have a gentle heart-to-heart to sort things out between you.

VII) SLAGS

We're studs, you're slags

A boy will often deal with a girl who he wants to put in her place by calling her a slag. It could be that she's a bit forward and pushy, or that she dresses provocatively, which makes him feel insecure, so he tries to make her and her mates (and, of course, *his* mates) think that he isn't intimidated.

Boys will also call a girl a slag if she's the type who flirts around without really meaning it, or if she's broken their heart. Boys don't give their affection easily, so if they should be unfortunate enough to fall for a girl who doesn't feel the same way, and she rejects him publicly, the way he'll salvage his pride is by saying "Well, she was a slag anyway. Who cares about her?".

The unfair thing in all of this is that a girl's reputation can be damaged when people go round calling her a slag. If, however, similar rumours fly around about a boy, he'll just get a hearty pat on the back from his mates, and get called a "stud"!

If it happens to you

If you choose to be quite feisty with boys, or to split up with someone you're sick of, you *don't* deserve to be called a slag, but it may still happen. So what do you do? Just ignore it for the pathetic nonsense that it is. The people that really matter to you won't be so stupid as to believe it.

However, if you've been flirting around without really meaning it, flirting when you already have a boyfriend, or generally toying with boys' affections, then you really are asking for trouble. This doesn't mean you're a slag, of course, but it does mean that the boys involved are going to find the easiest way of getting back at you, and they won't hesitate to make your life a misery. And once *they've* started, you often find that there are always some bitchy girls who'll just love to join in with the name-calling and try and "put you in your place". Be warned!

♥♥ D. GIRLS AS FRIENDS ♥♥

I) THE ADVANTAGES

No FEAR

Unlike boys' male mates, female chums are, on the whole, pretty safe to confide in. They know that they can discuss their true feelings and show their sensitive side without fear of ridicule. And what a huge relief it must be to say, "I think my girlfriend's gone off me – what can I do?" to someone without fear of having, "Carrie wants to chuck Paul!" sniggered loudly all over the school.

Whereas boys tend to be in constant – if unconscious – competition with each other – girls don't tend to be so desperate to compete in the same way, and this means that boys don't have to put on an act of bravado for a female friend.

Inside INFO

Befriending girls also means boys can find out a whole lot more about what makes the opposite sex tick. Rather than sitting around with their boy mates *guessing* what makes girls do what they do, with a girl mate boys can get an accurate explanation straight from the horse's mouth (so to speak). Answers to questions such as "How come she gets all huffy whenever I speak to my ex?" are more likely to be genuinely *useful* if they come from a girl who's quite possibly experienced the very same irrational feelings of jealousy when confronted with her beloved's former girlfriend. And, of course, *you* can learn a lot from *him* too.

Furthermore, mixed-sex friendships give easy access to each other's potentially fanciable mates. Mind you, if your boy pal seems to be slowly dating his way through all your mates while pretending to be all chummy with you, well the guy's a loser and no real friend to you. And that applies to you with *his* friends too.

II) ARE YOU JUST GOOD FRIENDS?

It's purely "Platonic"

A platonic relationship is one between a boy and a girl in which romance just doesn't feature, ie, a straightforward friendship. Now some boys – and girls – just do not believe that such a friendship can exist. In their eyes, a boy and a girl cannot be interested in each other without fancying each other. How very sad. The fact is, such friendships *are* possible between people who are sufficiently mature and honest to handle them.

The trouble is, when a lad befriends you, however honest and genuine his intentions as a chum may be, other people – especially his and your mates – can be utterly cynical about it. Your mates might say, "He's just pretending to be your friend so that you get close and then he can make a move on you." His mates undoubtedly say, "Go on, get in there – she's mad on you!" however innocent your interest in each other may be.

If you're chums with a lad and you have even the *teeniest* suspicion that his interest in you might be more than just platonic, you need to be very careful indeed. Just imagine what's going to happen when you start dating someone else; your so-called mate will be wild with jealousy! And you have to be equally honest with yourself about your feelings for him; if you're secretly in love with him but too scared to tell him how you feel, remaining "just good friends" might only upset you in the long run. Remember that if you do tell him how you feel and he doesn't feel the same way, once you've got it all out in the open you *can* still be friends as before. It's just a matter of being mature about it.

It has to be said that lads who befriend girls win a certain amount of (probably unspoken) admiration from their mates. They may scoff at the idea of platonic relationships, but in most cases they're just plain jealous of any lad who understands women so well that he can actually be friends with one without it being anything more. It also has to be said that such a lad in turn becomes immensely popular with his male mates, because through him they inevitably get to meet lots more girls!

More than friends

Befriending a boy is the very best way to get to know him. Not every single male friend is, necessarily, a potential boyfriend. Nor should you only befriend boys if you fancy them! But there are worse ways of choosing a boyfriend than by becoming really close friends first. Many girls say, "Oh, we were friends for ages and I didn't really see him in a romantic sense, but as I learnt to trust him, well I just ended up wanting us to be *more than friends...*"

If you quite fancy someone and start becoming pally, make sure that the friendship doesn't get so deep between you that it's impossible for you to see each other as anything other than a friend.

If you quite fancy someone, really like his personality, and want to get to know him better, well fine. But if, say, it transpires that he *only* sees you as a friend, you must take that in your stride and not go looking for something that's just not there. And if you find yourself going off your chum as a potential boyfriend, don't go dropping him like a hot potato – remember, you're friends, right? So no one's feelings need to be hurt.

SHE'S TOO SERIOUS

I started seeing Angie a couple of weeks ago, and although I really like her, she seems to want to get too serious too quickly. I mean, she seems to want us to spend all our time together and complains if I want to see my mates. What can I do?

Mick, 13

Dear Mick,

There's only one thing you can do – tell her exactly how you feel. Unfortunately some girls get a bit carried away when they're smitten, but there's absolutely no reason why you should go along with it. Tell her that you really like her but want to take the time to get to know her gradually. Make it clear that your friends mean a lot to you and that you don't want to have to make any huge sacrifices in order to keep her happy. If she won't respect your feelings and settle for some sort of a compromise, she's just being selfish and you'd be better off with someone else.

IN LOVE WITH MY FRIEND

I've been really good friends with Desley for over a year, and in spite of what everyone's said, it's always been just a friendship. But now she's got a boyfriend and suddenly I feel really jealous. I'm even starting to fancy her, and I want to tell her so. Am I really in love with her?

M, 16

Dear M,
Only you know the answer to that, but you definitely need to sort your emotions out once and for all before you talk to her about it! Friendships with a member of the opposite sex are a bit weird in that you've always got that thought in the back of your mind that you could one day go out together. Maybe you weren't even aware that that thought was there, but now she's met someone for herself, you can't stand the thought that she's out of bounds. But do you really fancy her? I suspect not. I can't help thinking that it's only now that someone else has decided she's fanciable that you've started to see the beauty in her. Give yourself the time to watch how your feelings towards her progress over the next few weeks and try not to let your feelings affect your friendship. In time you'll be able to see the difference between romantic love and platonic love and, hopefully, decide which of the two you feel for Desley.

SHE WANTS MY MATES

I've been best friends with this girl in my class since we were at primary school. She's really cute but I don't really fancy her – she's more like a sister to me. The problem is, I sometimes feel she just stays friends with me so she can get to know my mates. She only really talks to me if any fanciable friend of mine is around. She used to talk to me all the time. I feel so used.

Georgie, 15

Dear Georgie,
This girl's behaviour is very hurtful, and I'm not surprised you're feeling so miserable. But I bet she has no idea that she's being so rotten to you. Sometimes it's easy to forget the important things and take friends for granted, both male and female. It's very important that you let her know how she's making you feel. Tell her that you've always really valued her friendship but that now she seems to only have time for you when she thinks you might be able to help along her love life. Tell her you miss the laughs you two used to have and ask her if you could spend some time together without any of your male friends being involved. She might be a bit taken aback at first, but if you really matter to her, she'll soon realise how selfish she's been. And then you can get back to being good mates.

Section 3

FLIRTING AND FANCYING

A. HOW BOYS FLIRT

I) ATTENTION SEEKING

Teasing Bearing in mind the fact that boys fear rejection and humiliation more than a week-long appointment with the dentist, it goes without saying that their flirting techniques are indirect and a bit *useless.*

A favourite line is to tease you. Okay, we know that most boys tease girls anyway – it's one of those boring facts of life we just have to like or lump – but when it comes to girls they fancy, the teasing goes into *overdrive*. Every time they see you they'll start loudly joking about who you look like, who you fancy and how crap you look. What this really means is that they think you look brilliant and wish you fancied them!

Some will make very personal (and not very flattering) comments about your appearance. In some cases, this will turn into a nickname – "Blondie", "Big-Bum", "Madonna", (though you may not bear even a passing resemblance to her), "Hot-lips", or whatever else they can come up with. This nickname will be shouted or jeered at every possible occasion and repeated ad infinitum, usually accompanied by a huge smirk. Don't take offence, take heed; from the looks of it this boy fancies you *very much indeed*.

Insults Of course, if the teasing and name-calling starts to take on offensive proportions, then it's no fun at all. You can end up dreading encounters with this boy because he always shows you up and makes you cringe.

Think about why he's doing it. It could be that this boy isn't getting positive vibes from you and his pride's hurt so he's taking it out on you. It could be that he's just plain old insecure. Whatever the case, remember that you have a right not to fancy him back! If his teasing gets spiteful, don't try to be spiteful back – just have a sharp word with him. It's not your fault if you don't feel the same way, and he's just going to have to learn to take rejections like a man!

II) EYE TO EYE CONTACT

Peekaboo A favourite of the shy type and infinitely preferable to being bombarded with insults is the flirtation-by-staring technique. If you catch a boy looking at you frequently, or holding your gaze for just slightly longer than is normal, then looking away when you look at him, then returning his eyes to your face again – well, it's pretty darn likely that he's got a "thing" about you. This is a good way for him to a) let you know he likes you, b) find out if you like him too, and c) hopefully, avoid making a fool of himself in public. If you don't like him, just don't return his gaze. He'll soon get the message. If you do, then look right back at him and, when you're sure no one else is looking, give him a little smile. Don't overdo it, or he might just think you're laughing at him. Just a little grin should do the trick. Hopefully this will be sufficiently encouraging for him to go ahead and actually talk to you!

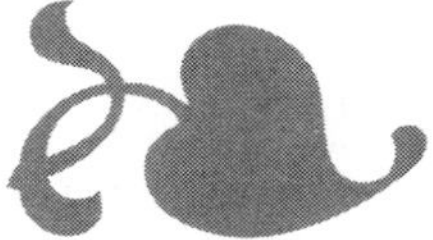

III) TEAMWORK

One of the crowd

Some lads don't mind their mates knowing who they fancy. In fact, some lads actually *prefer* to get their mates involved in their flirting because it's safety in numbers and, more crucially, they can set things up for each other.

A lad who fancies you might, for example, get his pals to get to know you so they can suss you out and try and find out if the feeling's mutual. They might sing his praises or, alternatively, slag him off, just to see what sort of a reaction this gets from you. Of course, it could be that a whole group of lads fancy you and your mates, but while they all know which of you they prefer, it might take some time for you to suss it out!

Basically, the team effort style of flirting can be a lot of fun as there's much less danger of anyone showing themselves up and feeling humiliated. And you can have a great laugh together in the process.

My Mate Fancies You

The coward's approach. Few chat-up lines in the history of flirting can be more frustrating than having some boy trot over and whisper, "My mate fancies you...". *Well why can't he tell me himself?* you feel like screaming. Because he's a bit useless, that's why.

But still, it *is* nice to find out that someone rather likes you, especially if the feeling's mutual. If the boy you like sends his mate over to declare his undying love (or attraction, at any rate), tell his mate to go back and tell him to come and ask you out in person. If he's not man enough to speak to you face-to-face, then he's not man enough to be your boyfriend, is he? Simple.

IV) SOME WAYS TO TELL HE FANCIES YOU

- ✌ He's always where you are.
- ♥ He's forever surreptitiously glancing in your direction.
- ✌ He seems to brighten up when you come in the room.
- ♥ Alternatively, he starts to show off!
- ✌ His mates nudge each other and him when you're there.
- ♥ He makes very personal comments about your appearance.
- ✌ He teases you about your supposedly dating/fancying other boys.
- ♥ He blushes when you look at him.
- ✌ When he talks to you, he can't quite look you in the eye.
- ♥ In conversation with you he brings up a little thing you told him weeks ago.
- ✌ He's forever asking, "Where's your boyfriend, then?".
- ♥ His eyes flash dangerously when you talk to other boys.

- He seems to know your every single move.
- He makes stupid jokes about your new haircut.
- He hangs around you, trying hard to make it look casual.
- He looks at your lips when he's talking to you.
- He and his mates come and dance right next to you at parties and show off to get your attention.
- He walks home your way, even though it's miles out of his way.
- He asks if you're okay when you've been off sick for a few days.
- He always manages to sit next to you whenever you're out

V) BODY LANGUAGE

A more subtle but often very reliable way of finding out whether or not a boy likes you is through his body language. These little tell-tale signs are great because they're made completely unconsciously, and if you know what to look for, they're a dead giveaway.

One body language trait that says, "I fancy you," is when a boy turns as much of his body towards you as possible when he's next to you. If he's sitting down, this means that, although he may be talking or listening to someone else, the rest of his body is still turned to you. He may also cross his legs and direct them towards you. Both these signs are very positive as they mean that he feels comfortable with you and likes what you're saying!

He may also preen himself while looking at or talking to you, touching his hair, straightening his shirt, gently scratching his face, etc, and this is his way of attracting your attention. If he sits directly facing you with his legs wide apart and his hands on his upper thighs, he's not only sexually attracted to you, but he's also pretty confident that you fancy him too! He might also push his shoulders back and flex his muscles (if he's got any!) for you to admire.

QUIZ

VI) DOES HE FANCY YOU?

Okay, you've met a boy you like, you can't stop thinking about him day and night, and you've just got to get to know him. But does he feel the same way? There's only one sure way to find out...

1. When you walk into a room, is he more likely to...

a. *Shout "Oi, that's my future wife, that is!" pointing straight at you.*
b. *Smile at you then look away.*
c. *Ignore you completely and talk to all your mates.*
d. *Start telling you about his new computer game.*

2. For your birthday party, he...

a. *Goes away for the weekend.*
b. *Offers to give you a birthday kiss and calls you "Grandma" all evening.*
c. *Gives you a jokey card with a very silly message.*
d. *Waits till you're on your own to give you a little card simply signed with his name and a couple of x's.*

3. Still at your party, another lad who you seriously don't like starts very insistently chatting you up. Does the boy you fancy ...

a. *Start chatting someone else up.*
b. *Come over and say, "Sorry to interrupt, mate, but it's time to give the birthday girl 'the bumps.'"*
c. *Looks like he wants to beat him up.*
d. *Hang around keeping half an eye on the situation, then come over to rescue you when the other guy gets a bit heavy.*

QUIZQUIZQUIZ

4. You bump into him in your local shopping precinct on Saturday afternoon. Is he most likely to ...

a. Ask you the time and keep you talking for a bit.

b. Run a mile.

c. Keep you talking for ages and try to find out what you're doing later that evening.

d. Ask you to come and try the new game in the amusement arcade.

5. You've just had your hair style changed quite dramatically. When he sees you he ...

a. Doesn't even notice, he's too busy ranting on about the new Blur album.

b. Says, "Oh you've had your hair cut! It's, er, nice...", then changes the subject.

c. Laughs in your face.

d. Laughs, calls you "Baldy", says he'll beat up the hairdresser for you, then apologises profusely when you get offended.

6. When you have a conversation he's most likely to...

a. Interrupt you constantly and hardly let you get a word in edgeways.

b. Lean in really close and whisper lots of really personal questions.

c. Joke endlessly, and punch your shoulder every time he gets to a punchline.

d. Listen very intently to what you're saying, looking at either your eyes or your lips.

7. His mates are...

a. Really friendly towards you, just like he is, but they do tend to tease you both about your friendship.

b. Total strangers to you.

c. Always watching you and whispering and nudging each other whenever he's around.

d. Forever jeering at you and calling you his bird.

8. If you were to ask him out, you honestly, in your heart of hearts, reckon his reaction would be to...

a. Kiss you passionately on the spot.

b. Drop his Coke can on the spot and stammer with embarrassment.

c. Blush, smile and say yes.

d. Sneer and say, "I don't think so...".

1.	a. 15	b. 10	c. 0	d. 5
2.	a. 0	b.15	c. 5	d. 10
3.	a. 0	b. 5	c. 15	d. 10
4.	a. 10	b. 0	c. 15	d. 5
5.	a. 5	b. 10	c. 0	d. 15
6.	a. 0	b. 15	c. 5	d. 10
7.	a. 5	b. 0	c. 10	d. 15
8.	a. 15	b. 5	c. 10	d. 0

95-120

Make no mistake, this boy fancies you very much – as if you hadn't worked that one out for yourself! He's pretty blatant about it, so obviously he's quite confident of success, but he may also be the type who goes round fancying loads of girls and breaking plenty of hearts, so don't make things too easy for him. Let him chase you for a bit, and then, if you really like him, give him a break. But be careful!

65-90

Yes indeed, it sounds like he definitely has a bit of a thing for you, but he's also pretty shy and unsure of himself. So he's being subtle about it, to give him the chance to get to know you and try and work out if you fancy him back, without making too much of a fool of himself. Just a bit more gentle encouragement is all that's needed on your part to get you two together!

35-60

Hmm, not so clear, this one. He sees you and treats you very much as a mate, someone he can have a good laugh with without feeling threatened. And that's brilliant, because not all girls manage to befriend a boy the way you have. He obviously respects you and values your company. But there may be more to it than that – maybe this friendship business is just a way of getting close to you so he can check you out!

0-30

Hate to be the one to have to break it to you, but this boy is not interested in you in the slightest. We've heard of playing it cool, but if he played it any cooler he'd freeze over! Nope, he's obviously got his eyes on someone else, and there's not a lot you can do about it. But hey, why waste your time on a boy who doesn't fancy you? Find yourself one you like who happens to like you back!

10 ways to get a boy to notice you

- ♥ Smile broadly at him when you see him.
- ♥ Ask him about himself. He'll be flattered that you're interested in him.
- ♥ When you look at him, discreetly hold your gaze on him until he notices, then turn away the second he looks at you.
- ♥ Be interested in, and have an opinion on, whatever he has to say.
- ♥ Tease him. But no more than he teases you!
- ♥ Laugh loudly in his presence. Especially at his jokes!
- ♥ Tell him about the things that make you happy. It'll make him feel closer to you.
- ♥ Ask him if he's going out with anyone at the moment. A bit bold, this one!
- ♥ Touch his arm when you talk to him and look intently into his eyes.
- ♥ Moan a bit about how useless boys are when it comes to dating. This is a last resort!

Boys to avoid

- Boys who two-time
- Boys who gossip to all and sundry about how far they've gone with whom
- Boys who're more interested in impressing their mates by going out with you than in getting to know you
- Boys who'll only talk to you when the two of you are on your own
- Boys who're always drinking, being crude and getting into fights
- Boys who try to touch you in places where you don't want to be touched
- Boys who don't make sure that you get home safely after you've been out with them
- Boys who aren't interested in hearing what you think or feel
- Boys who're constantly eyeing up other girls
- Boys who try to persuade you to have sex against your will

10 ways to get a boy to run a mile

- ✘ Look at him adoringly all the time.
- ✘ Agree with every single thing he says, and never offer an opinion of your own.
- ✘ Let it be known throughout your whole school that you adore him.
- ✘ Hang around outside his house, checking out his every move.
- ✘ Bombard him with love notes and little gifts.
- ✘ Beat up any other girl who so much as looks at him.
- ✘ Get your mates to ask him why he doesn't like you.
- ✘ Talk to him constantly about your ex-boyfriends.
- ✘ Say: "You should see my cousin's baby – she's *sooooo* sweet!"
- ✘ Ask if he wants to nip down to the jeweller's with you to look at the rings.

B. ASKING OUT

I) SUSSING YOU OUT

What he says, what he means

These are a few of the little tricks boys will use to suss out if you're available and interested in them, before putting themselves through the indignity of asking you out!

He says: "Are you going to Jackie's party?"
He means: "I hope so, because I am"

He says: "Where's your boyfriend tonight?"
He means: "Have you got a boyfriend?"

He says (pretending to look annoyed): "Oh I might have known you'd turn up..."
He means: "I'm really glad you did!"

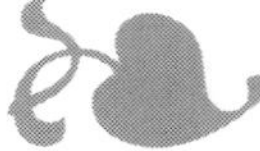

He says: "Don't I know you from somewhere?"
He means: "I've never seen you before, but this is the only way I can think of to get you talking!"

He says: "You can't walk home on your own – anything could happen!"
He means: "If anything's going to happen, it's me kissing you!"

He says: "You must be cold. Here, borrow my jacket."
He means: "I'm just looking for an excuse to have to come round to your house tomorrow."

He says: "Do you always come here?"

He means: "Make sure you do in future."

He says: "Oh, I expect you're busy tomorrow night..."
He means: "If you say you aren't, I just might have the guts to ask you out!"

He says: "Come here, I need to talk to you about something"
He means: "Come here, I want to get you out of everyone's hearing distance, and if you agree to, I'll know you like me."

He says (on seeing you talking to another boy): "Oooh, looks like you've got an admirer there!"
He means: "I'm jealous – do you like him back?"

10 phrases which mean "Will you go out with me?"

- ♥ What would you say if I asked you out?
- ♥ Let's make a go of it...
- ♥ Can I say you're my girlfriend?
- ♥ Shall we get together sometime?
- ♥ Let's be more than just friends
- ♥ Do you want my phone number?
- ♥ Will you come down here next week?
- ♥ Jim said you like me...
- ♥ When can I see you again?
- ♥ Shall I phone you one day?

II) ASKING YOU OUT

What goes through his head

Picture the scene. He's fancied you from afar. He's got to know as much as he can about you, without making a spectacle of himself. And now there's nothing else for it. He has to ask you out. The thought of uttering those, "Will you go out with me?" words fill him with dread.

What if she says no? Or worse, what if she laughs in my face? She might go and tell everyone I asked her out! What if she's too embarrassed to say no? If she says she'd rather just be friends, I'll die on the spot...

These fears explain why it takes some boys so long to get round to it. As far as you're concerned, you've given him tons of encouragement and, short of wearing a sign saying, "Go on – ask me out, you fool!" you've done all you can to help things along. But he's still stalling, and you're beginning to wonder if you've read the signs wrong. Patience. He'll get round to it eventually.

Whatever you do, don't a) laugh; b) tell him to spit it out; or c) yell, "Hey everybody, Mark's about to pop the question!". Just smile encouragingly and chat to him to put him at his ease. Or, if you really think it's just never going to happen, you may have to take matters into your own hands...

III) ASKING HIM OUT

What they think of it

"What do I think of girls asking me out? It's brilliant. It's really flattering and it takes the pressure off us lads."

Simon, 15

Virtually all boys *love* being asked out. It flatters their egos, makes them feel fancied and makes life infinitely easier for them. And, unlike a few years back when it was considered brash and unfeminine for a girl to do the asking, these days it's becoming more and more acceptable – so much so, that some boys have got a bit lazy about the whole thing and fully *expect* girls to deal with it!

There are some rather unkind boys who consider girls who ask them out to be desperate and even a bit "easy", but these are in a minority, and they're usually pretty easy to spot. And while you certainly shouldn't let yourself be put off by that possibility, it's definitely worth getting to know the boy you want to date before you ask him out, to make sure that a) you really like him, and b) that he's not a rotter who'll only take advantage of your fancying him!

When they can't say NO

Some girls worry that if they ask a boy out he might be too embarrassed to say no, which means they'll end up going out with someone who doesn't really fancy them. Well, yes, this *can* happen, but, just like girls, most boys know deep down that it's better to disappoint someone sooner rather than later and say no *straight away*!

I mean, if someone asked you out and you really didn't fancy them, how would you react? Okay, you'd feel flattered, but you'd still say no (albeit in the nicest way possible), wouldn't you?

How to do IT

We've established the importance of getting to know your intended chap, but once you've decided that he is definitely the one for you, and feel reasonably sure that he'd like things to go further too, here's what you have to do.

Next time you're together, say something like, "I quite fancy seeing Keanu's new sci-fi film, *Johnny Mnemonic* – do you want to come with me?". Chances are, he might say, "Um, no, I've already seen it..." in which case you should just reply, "Oh okay, well, maybe another time...". This gives him the chance, if he does like you, to say something like, "But I've got *Reality Bites* on video... do you fancy popping over to see it?". Or not, as the case may be.

The main thing is not to let the conversation get *pressurised.* Think out roughly what you're going to say beforehand. Don't go into a sulk or get upset if he doesn't seem to be responding, and try not to let your nerves get the better of you. Boys need a certain amount of time before they can get the hang of being chatted up, so don't despair if he's not getting the message!

Do not...

- Get your best mate to ask him for you
- Get *his* best mate to ask him for you
- Ask him in front of an audience
- Blurt out, "Do you want to go out with me?" then run away
- Cry in front of him if he says no
- Say, "Now you don't *have* to say yes or anything, and I'm sure you have something better to do, but..."
- Beg if he says no
- Ask him something completely unlikely, like whether he wants to go ballroom dancing with you
- Accuse him of fancying someone else
- Tell him he's crap if he doesn't seem to have got the message

IS HE A MATCH FOR YOU?

Try to find out the star sign of the boy you fancy. How close is he to his star sign character? Do you fancy boys you're supposed to be compatible with?

ARIES
TAURUS
GEMINI
CANCER
LEO
VIRGO
LIBRA
SCORPIO
SAGITTARIUS
CAPRICORN
AQUARIUS
PISCES

THE ARIES BOY

What he's like:

The Arien boy is loud, up front and usually pretty popular. Full of charm and surprises, he's the kind that a lot of girls find hard to resist. He's confident almost to the point of arrogance and extremely sociable. You'd never be bored with this boy, but you might get a bit fed up with him wanting his own way all the time!

He's compatible with:

Gemini, Leo and Sagittarius.

How he'll try to get you:

By saying, "Hey babe, tonight's your lucky night!" This one's not shy in the least and he's totally fearless of rejection, because he knows his cheeky charm hardly ever fails.

How to get him:

You have to be as up-front with this boy as he is with you. Let him know in no uncertain terms that you fancy him, and if he fancies you back he'll soon grab the opportunity to ask you out. Ariens can't resist flattery!

Be warned:

He might try and take over your life.

THE TAURUS BOY

What he's like:

This one is affectionate and loyal, and well into security and steady relationships. He's quite stubborn and tough on the outside, but deep down he's well slushy and romantic, if only you have the patience to get beyond his bullish exterior. Once he's fallen in love with you, you can rely on him to stick with you for a very long time.

He's compatible with:

Cancer, Virgo and Capricorn.

How he'll try to get you:

This one's pretty slow on the uptake if someone's giving him, "I fancy you," signals, and he's pretty hopeless at chatting girls up too. One thing's for sure: he won't try anything at all unless he's been given plenty of encouragement!

How to get him:

If you like him, it's pretty much all up to you. Show interest in all he has to say, let him know by subtle means that you think he's fab and really get to know him. And don't be afraid to ask him out – he's a pushover when it comes to up-front girls!

Be warned:

He's got a bit of a temper!

THE GEMINI BOY

What he's like:

This boy's charismatic, sociable and great fun. He's also very fickle, which means that while you'll never feel like yawning when you're with him, you'll sometimes wonder why the hell you're involved! Basically, you may have to put up with a lot from him, so only pursue this one if you're totally smitten!

He's compatible with:

Leo, Libra and Aquarius.

How he'll try to get you:

By climbing a tree, pretending to fall off, sprawling flat at your feet and declaring undying love until you're in fits of laughter. How could you resist?

How to get him:

Make him laugh and show him that you're just as much of a buffoon as he is. He loves to be with someone who can entertain him and keep him interested, while keeping up with his ever-changing moods.

Be warned:

He can't resist flirting with other girls.

THE CANCER BOY

What he's like:

He's extremely fussy when it comes to girls and won't go out with just anyone. However, once he's hooked, this one is sincerity itself, so if he says something, he means it. This means he can be quite tactless at times, but at least you know where you are! He's also quite prone to irritability, which can be a bind, but his endearingly bumbling ways will still win you over.

He's compatible with:

Virgo, Scorpio and Pisces.

How he'll try to get you:

Through long and intense conversations, during which time he'll try and strike up a special bond with you. This may take some time!

How to get him:

Concentrate on impressing him with your depth. Let him know that he's found his soul-mate, that you're 100 per cent trust-worthy and will always take him and his thoughts seriously. And make sure you do!

Be warned:

He'll never forget it if you hurt him.

THE LEO BOY

What he's like:

Your Leo chap is a gregarious and fun-loving type with a huge ego and need for attention. He's immensely popular and generous, involving everyone around him in his high jinks, and he particularly loves a female audience. He's also a bit of a show-off and rather fond of his appearance.

He's compatible with:

Libra, Sagittarius and Aries.

How he'll try to get you:

By impressing you with his looks, flash clothes and glamorous lifestyle. Be prepared to get swept off your feet!

How to get him:

This one's a sucker for compliments, so if you pay him heaps of attention and let him know he's fab, he'll be yours. And don't be afraid to be forthright about it, because Leo boys really admire strong girls.

Be warned:

Looks really count for this one.

THE VIRGO BOY

What he's like

This one's Mr Organised and will rarely do anything without carefully weighing up the pros and cons. He's got a great sense of humour and a very loving, protective nature, but he does tend to find fault with everything, which can be a bit tiresome!

He's compatible with:

Scorpio, Capricorn and Taurus.

How he'll try to get you

By finding out all there is to know about you and biding his time until the exact right moment comes along to make a play for you. This "play for you" may *almost* happen a few times before you get fed up and end up asking him out yourself!

How to get him

Get him talking about his problems and be hugely sympathetic and understanding. Boost his ego and be supportive of his every whim. He'll soon find that you've become indispensable to his life!

Be warned:

He can be a bit of a grump!

THE LIBRA BOY

What he's like:

This one knows how to charm the girls and no mistake. He's cheeky and naughty, but somehow he gets away with it, just by flashing you that "you love me really" grin. He's also incredibly indecisive, which can be frustrating, not to mention his annoying tendency to be a bit superficial.

He's compatible with:

Sagittarius, Aquarius and Gemini.

How he'll try to get you:

By charming you until you succumb to his irresistible charm. Watch out – he'll get right under your skin!

How to get him:

As he's always in a relationship, you'll have to pay close attention to his love life so that when his next relationship ends, you can jump in there! Then simply tell him that he's going out with you whether he likes it or not – he just loves bossy girls.

Be warned:

He's not very good at making commitments.

THE SCORPIO BOY

What he's like:

This one's a pretty thrilling person to know, in spite of – or maybe *because* of – the fact that he can be positively dangerous when it comes to toying with people's emotions. He's clever and witty and highly perceptive, which gives him the power to play games with people – something he loves to do.

He's compatible with:

Capricorn, Pisces and Cancer.

How he'll try to get you:

If this one wants you, he's going to get you, make no mistake! He'll intrigue you by telling you things about yourself that you'd never even admitted to yourself, and next thing you know, you're hypnotised!

How to get him:

Play it very cool. Find out everything you can about him so that when you have a conversation, *you* can impress *him* with your deep insights!

Be warned:

He absolutely *has* to be in control.

THE SAGITTARIUS BOY

What he's like:

He's a total scream and loves to hear the sound of his own voice and be the centre of attention. In fact, he's such a character that some people find him a bit too much to keep up with. He can't meet a girl without flirting, so don't get too excited if he switches the charm on for you!

He's compatible with:

Aquarius, Aries and Leo.

How he'll try to get you:

This one doesn't have to try – flirting comes naturally to Mr Sagittarius. He'll just be loud and charming and embarrass you until you give up all resistance.

How to get him:

Just get his attention – he'll do the rest! The only problem is *keeping* his attention once you've got it!

Be warned:

He may well break your heart.

THE CAPRICORN BOY

What he's like:

Not the most thrilling of people at first glance, the Capricorn boy is in fact a real sweetheart. He's extremely sensitive and loving, and totally reliable. It might bug you that he's so sensible and careful in everything he does, but he'll grow on you just by exuding his calm, quiet self-assuredness.

He's compatible with:

Pisces, Taurus and Virgo.

How he'll try to get you:

By always being there, always being nice and basically waiting to see if he can get you to fall for him.

How to get him:

Unfortunately you'll never know for sure if he fancies you, so you're going to have to take your courage in both hands and ask him out. But this boy's so sweet and reassuring, it'll be a breeze.

Be warned:

He's a bit obsessed with his hobbies.

THE AQUARIUS BOY

What he's like:
He's clever, deep, and a bit of a dreamer – in fact, you'll sometimes wonder if you inhabit the same planet! His cleverness makes him very funny and weird but a bit aloof, and this coolness can mean any girlfriend of his ends up feeling a bit neglected.

He's compatible with:
Aries, Gemini and Libra.

How he'll try to get you:
By starting an intellectual conversation which will, hopefully, assure him once and for all that you're his type.

How to get him:
Show him that you're as self-contained and cool as he is and have in-depth knowledge of his favourite conversational subjects. And smile!

Be warned:
He can't stand superficiality and gossip.

THE PISCES BOY

What he's like:

This one's a hopeless romantic with a heart of gold. He's quite prone to soppiness and helpless adoration which can be a bit much, especially if he puts you on a pedestal. He's also a bit of a dreamer and hence totally impractical. However, he's sweetness itself and would never hurt you.

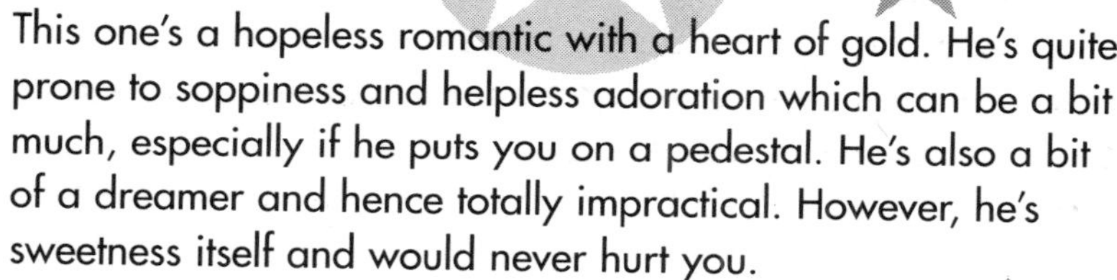

He's compatible with:

Taurus, Cancer and Scorpio.

How he'll try to get you:

He sees you as a goddess, so he'll look at you in an awestruck, admiring fashion until you're sucked into his irresistible softness.

How to get him:

This is one of the few star signs that responds to love poetry! Write your feelings down in dreamy rhyme and he'll soon be smitten.

Be warned:

Handle with care – he's very easily hurt.

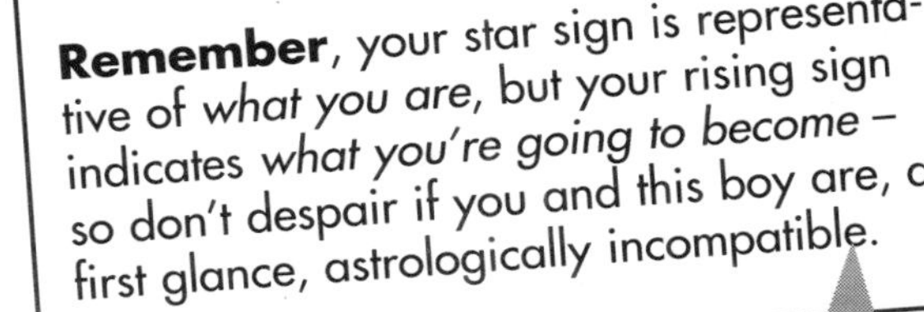

Remember, your star sign is representative of *what you are*, but your rising sign indicates *what you're going to become* – so don't despair if you and this boy are, at first glance, astrologically incompatible.

I DON'T KNOW HOW TO ASK HER out

Me and this girl at school are always giving each other the eye but I don't really know what to do next. She told my friend that she likes me and he told her that I like her, and we're always teasing each other, but I just don't know where to take it from here.

Jon, 13

Dear Jon,
Well there's certainly no doubt about the fact that she fancies you! You're obviously inexperienced with girls, and there's nothing wrong with that, but somehow you need to find the confidence to move onto the next step. The best thing you can do is get to know each other. Next time you see her, don't just tease her, but stop and chat for a bit, just briefly. It doesn't really matter what about – someone you both know, maybe – anything to get the conversation going. If you get into the habit of making chitchat in this way, it should be easy from there to mention a party or night out that you're going to soon and suggest that she could come along too. She may well jump at the chance.

WHY DOES SHE FLIRT WITH ME?

I'm in love with Janine, a girl who hangs around with my cousin. Although she's three years older than me , she's always flirting with me, and I'm always flirting back. Recently she started going out with someone in her year, but one night when she was drunk she let me kiss her. I've given her loads of presents and even asked her out, but she says she's no good for me. Why does she flirt with me? I'm so confused.

Neil, 14

Dear Neil,

This girl's absolutely right, she's no good for you at all. She obviously does find you attractive and enjoys the attention you shower on her, but at the same time, for whatever reason, she doesn't want there to be more between you than a bit of teasing. It's wrong of her to toy with your affections like this, especially when you're so much younger than her and when she already has a boyfriend, so however hard you may find it, try not to take her flirting too seriously. I know how painful it is for you to deal with her mixed messages, but trying to make more of this than just a flirty friendship will only lead to more heartache for you. Try not to be alone with this girl again, and don't try to kiss her, however tempting it may be.

Section 4

I) THE FIRST DATE

What to wear

Believe it or not, lads agonize over what to wear on a first date just as much as girls do. They might not spend *quite* so long trying things on – and they may well end up wearing the top they've been wearing all day – but they still fret and worry about looking right and smelling nice.

It's not as easy for a lad to transform himself into sheer loveliness the way girls can. All it takes for you is the right outfit plus a quick blow-dry, a slick of lipstick and a coating of mascara and bingo, you're beautiful. Lads, on the other hand, will play close attention to (and stress over) spots, razor nicks and blemishes – if they're daring they might even borrow their sister's spot-stick – and apply aftershave liberally to mask any body odours due to the stressfulness of the situation!

It's pretty scary

Lads view dates with a mixture of excitement and *trepidation*. The problem is, they feel that so much is expected of them. They're meant to know of somewhere cool to go, and be able to think of heaps of interesting and amusing things to say, and if they don't then they feel like a failure. And this makes them panic!

Lads on the whole aren't as good at making conversation as girls, so they feel instantly inadequate in such situations, and they're not too sure what makes girls tick, so they don't really know where to begin. This is why it's an excellent idea to really get to know each other before you go on a date!

Boys also worry that you'll expect instantly to become girlfriend and boyfriend after the first date. You may be thinking nothing of the sort, but if you *are*, don't expect the lad in question to enthuse when you make it quite obvious that you assume that you'll be inseparable from this point onwards. Remember, a date is a chance for you to get to know each other on your own and see if you really like each other. It's best not to assume *anything at all* at this stage.

To **kiss** or not to **kiss**?

If your date goes well and you're getting on brilliantly, you might wonder if he's going to kiss you. Let's get one thing straight. If he *does* kiss you, it doesn't mean that you're as good as married. And if he *doesn't* kiss you at the end of the night, it doesn't mean that he can't stand you, thinks you're hideous and doesn't want to see you again. Think about it. It takes guts to just steam in there and kiss a girl, however much he may like you and you like him. In fact, sometimes, the more he likes you, the more nervous he gets about that very first mouth-to-mouth moment!

All the time you're thinking, *"Is he going to kiss me? Doesn't he like me? I must've been reading his signals all wrong. Is he too shy? He obviously thinks I'm too ugly... Maybe I should try and kiss him..."*, a similar scenario's running through his head. *"Do I kiss her now? I'm not sure she wants me to. How can I know for sure? She might slap me if I try! Will she think I'm a wimp if I don't? I don't know how to get that close to her without being really obvious and making a fool of myself,"* etc, etc.

CUTE BOY PLOYS

To get you close enough to kiss

- Yawning and stretching so that his arm just sort of "accidentally" lands on your shoulder.
- Saying, "C'mere, I wanna tell you something, but I have to whisper it..." to get you in kissing proximity.
- Saying, "What colour are your eyes again? Let's have a closer look..." so that you have to face him and meet his gaze.
- Insisting that your neck's all tense and you need a shoulder rub. Careful with this one – massage can be very seductive!
- Pretending to be so intoxicated with your perfume that he just *has* to get a closer whiff, so he can start nuzzling your neck!
- Saying, "Aren't you cold? You look *freezing...*" so he's got an excuse to put his arm round you and keep you warm.
- Pretending to have something in his eye, so that you rush to his aid and have to get your face close to his in order to inspect the damage.
- Asking you for a slow dance, to get his arms round your waist and yours round his neck.
- Whispering the words of the smoochy song right next to your ear, to get you all tingly and swoony (*tremble*).
- Saying, "Does that lipstick smudge?" then grinning enigmatically till you ask him why, so that he can *show* you his reason... with his lips!

On a first date, do...

- ✔ Remember that he's probably nervous too, so make allowances.
- ✔ Think of some easy subjects to talk about to help things along. Stuff like what's happening in the Soaps, a film you've just seen, a band you know he likes, etc.
- ✔ Wear something that's pretty much what he's used to seeing you wear – outrageous slinky gear and teetering high heels will only make you feel self-conscious and him more nervous.
- ✔ Say something complimentary – everyone likes to be flattered and it'll put him at his ease.
- ✔ Suggest something cheap to do, in case he's broke but too embarrassed to say so.
- ✔ Smile and laugh at his jokes, so you can both relax.
- ✔ If you notice his knees are still shaking, tell him that you're feeling nervous – he might feel a bit less intimidated!
- ✔ Ask him about himself, his mates, his hobbies, etc.
- ✔ At the end of the night, let him know you had a nice time (only if you did, of course!).
- ✔ When you're saying goodnight, lean forward to kiss him on the cheek. With any luck he might turn round and kiss you on the mouth!

On a first date do not...

- ✘ Take your best mate along for company.
- ✘ Talk constantly about your ex-boyfriends and how much you hate/still love them.
- ✘ Call him, "Darling," or say, "Now that you're my boyfriend, blah, blah..."
- ✘ Expect him to pay for everything.
- ✘ Arrive late, if you can help it!
- ✘ Yawn constantly and keep looking at your watch, even if you *are* having a boring time.
- ✘ Tell him he's a useless dresser/dancer/conversationalist.
- ✘ Talk about what your friends think of him.
- ✘ Talk about all the people you fancy.
- ✘ Ask him why his last girlfriend dumped him.

II) BOYS AND KISSING

What boys think about kissing

Most boys like kissing. Yes, just like girls, they can really get into those tongue-tingly, smoochy sensations – in fact, some of them will quite happily kiss for hours! And, like you, they feel very apprehensive before doing it for the first time. Even more than you, they feel like they should just *know* how to do it (and how *not* to do it), just because they think boys are meant to know these things. But they don't. Just like you, they can only guess how to do it by watching people kissing in films and by practising on the back of their hand – yes, boys do that too! Only you can bet they'd be far more *loathe* to admit it than you might be, and they'd certainly think twice before asking for kissing advice from their mates!

As a result of this snogging ignorance, some boys have a tendency to rush at their first kiss and make a bit of a hash of it. They're so worried about getting it wrong that they just lunge in there and get it over with as quickly as possible. The only thing you can do in this situation is be a bit patient and (if you're a slightly more confident kisser) gently get him to slow down and then show him how it's done.

More than kissing

You might think that all boys see kissing as a prelude to more heavy stuff, like fumbling around under your jumper, and so forth. But a lot of boys actually don't want to get into all that stuff. At least, not just yet. They're as nervous and worried as you are about "taking things further" (however self-assured they may pretend to be), and feel much happier sticking on safe snogging ground.

There are those, of course, who think that if you let them kiss you then you'll let them do anything! But these can soon be spotted by the way they develop Wandering Hand Disease as soon as the kissing commences. If a boy isn't happy just kissing when you've made it very plain that that's all you want to do, then he's probably not the boy for you. A boy worth having is one who respects your feelings, *whatever* his may be, so don't let yourself be persuaded to go further than you want just to keep your boy's interest.

How to get him to kiss you

Some boys can be pretty shy about kissing, especially if you happen to be their first girlfriend. However much they may like the idea of it, and really fancy you, they worry that they're going to do it all wrong and *disappoint* you, making a fool of themselves into the bargain. Of course, if you've just met or it's your first date, he may have the added worry of not knowing for sure whether or not you like him and actually *want* to be kissed. Poor thing!

This is where you can help. It could be that he just needs a bit of encouragement, a sign that you really would like to be kissed by him. If you haven't touched so far, just holding his hand or squeezing his arm could do the trick. Or, if you're sitting down, lean your head on his shoulder. Basically the key here is proximity. Once you're really close to each other, it can only be a matter of time before he feels confident enough to seek out your lips with his!

HOW to Kiss

If you've never been kissed before, you might be wondering just how on earth it's done and what it feels like.

Can it possibly feel nice? Is there a wrong way and a right way? Do you use tongues or not? How on earth can it be pleasant to swap spit and tongues with someone? Yeeeuch!

Well, rest assured, kissing is a very pleasant pastime indeed, if you happen to be doing it with someone you really like! Everyone will tell you that there is no set way to do it, and that you'll know instinctively what to do when the time comes. While that may be true, there are certain things you can do to help things along.

10 tips for a perfect kissing

One: Turn your head at an angle to his (so your noses won't bump).

Two: Now put your lips against his, slightly opening your mouth at the same time.

Three: Shut your eyes so neither of you feel self-conscious. Hopefully he'll do the same.

Four: Now slowly and gently begin to move your mouth rhythmically against his, slightly opening and closing it and getting your movements in sync with his.

Five: Gently suck his lips with yours as you kiss.

Six: If you're feeling more confident, slip your tongue into his mouth for a second, and if he responds by doing the same, it's your cue to explore each other's mouths with your tongues. Sounds revolting, but it's not!

Seven: Vary the speed and pressure of your kissing, slowing down to almost a stop and kissing really gently, then speeding up and getting fast and passionate. Oo-er!

Eight: If you're feeling really confident, pull away for a bit and gently nibble his lower lip.

Nine: When you want to finish, gradually slow down, then move off his mouth to his neck and plant a few little kisses there too.

Ten: Practise some of the previous steps on the back of your hand to see how it feels and get a bit more confident before you go for the real thing. Best do it in the privacy of your room, though!

10 kissing no-no's

One: Don't go too fast. It's unromantic and you might end up clashing teeth or bumping noses – not nice at all.

Two: Don't stick your tongue straight in his mouth. Let things build up gradually, and do everything gently.

Three: Don't keep your eyes open. He'll feel even more self-conscious if he thinks you're inspecting him from such close quarters.

Four: Don't try and breathe through your mouth! That's what your nose is there for.

Five: Don't stash your gum somewhere in your mouth – it might be a bit revolting for him to find out he's chewing your gum as well as snogging you!

Six: Don't dribble all over him. If there's too much saliva in your mouth, break off, swallow discreetly, then continue!

Seven: Don't smoke. You'll taste like an ash-tray, which is a huge turn-off. And it's a harmful and disgusting habit anyway!

Eight: Don't just open your mouth and let him do all the snogging. It's a two-way thing, you know!

Nine: Don't just break away abruptly when you've finished. Nuzzle his neck and give him a big hug instead.

Ten: Don't say "Eurgh, that was disgusting!" afterwards – even if it was!

A few comments from the boys...

"I like it when a girl starts kissing me rather than waiting for me to make the first move. Then I know she really likes me."

Kyle, 14

"Kissing's really nice if you're with the right person. When that happens I could keep kissing for hours."

Jerome, 13

"I think girls like kissing much more than boys do. Personally, I think it's boring."

Angus, 14

"I was so nervous about my first kiss that I had to ask my sister's advice on how to do it. But once I actually got round to it, it all came naturally, just like she said it would."

Jason, 12

"Once I kissed a girl who lunged at me and stuck her tongue straight down my throat before I knew what was happening. It was revolting."

Rob, 14

"Some girls wear so much lipstick, that it puts me right off kissing them. I just imagine getting it all over my face and my mates laughing at me!"

Ged, 15

III) AFTER THE FIRST DATE

What happens next

After a first date, lads will often say "I'll call you," or, "See you soon". They're rarely more specific than that, so it's difficult to guess exactly when that phone call or next encounter might take place, but that's okay – you've merely spent the evening getting to know each other, remember?

Some lads won't say anything apart from, "See ya, then..." at the end of a date, which could mean they're just being a bit cool and nonchalant, but fully intend to see you again. Alternatively, it could mean that they don't want to have a relationship. Basically, you can't push these things, so all you can do is think about whether or not *you* like *him* enough to see him again, and if you do, sit tight and hope for the best.

This, of course, can be torture. The will-he-won't-he-phone-me thoughts fill your head all day long, however much you try to push them out. So before you drive your friends and family mad with your wailing and moaning, if you can bear to do it (and risk possible rejection), take a deep breath and phone *him*. At least then you'll know where you stand.

Meanwhile, bear in mind the fact that most lads are hopeless on the phone, and can never think of a thing to say when they call you. Also, consider the fact that they really don't realise that while they're biding their time, you're in total torment waiting for that call. There are no strict rules about how long he should leave it before phoning you, but I think we can safely say that if he leaves it for much over a week, he can't be that interested.

When he doesn't phone

"I don't understand why boys say they'll phone you then don't bother. Do they get some kind of cruel kick out of it?"

Anna, 14

10 Reasons why he might not phone

"Sometimes I'll ask a girl for her number and then not get round to phoning her. I suppose I just chicken out."

Robert, 14

"Sometimes it just slips my mind."

Andy, 16

"If I ring straight away then I'll seem too keen, which is uncool. Then if I leave it too long, I daren't phone her in case she's annoyed and tells me to get lost."

Matthew, 15

"Saying I'll phone is just the easiest way to end an evening without anyone getting upset."

Kev, 13

"When I say I'll phone a girl I always mean it at the time, but then I talk myself out of it. So many things could go wrong."

Babs, 17

"I'm always taking girls' numbers without any intention of phoning them. It's fun and anyway, they know the score."

Karl, 16

"I don't want the girl to get too serious about me, because then she might want to see me every night. So sometimes I just don't get round to it."

Jaymal, 15

"I'm not very good on the phone and I can't think of anything to say, so I just don't bother."

Rich, 14

"Girls are always giving me their numbers, and I don't like to refuse. But there's no way I'm ringing a girl I don't fancy!"

Felix, 15

"If I've spent some time talking to a girl, I never really know how to leave it, so I always ask for her number out of politeness. I suppose I don't want to hurt her feelings."

Ed, 16

As you can see, there are plenty of reasons why boys don't always phone you when they say they will, but whatever his excuse may be, it's still not very nice, at the end of the day, to inflict this disappointment on someone. If a boy says he'll phone you and then doesn't, it's really important that you realise that it's not your fault. Don't go thinking, "Oh, he hasn't phoned me because I'm too fat/ugly/boring" or whatever, because more often than not, the reason that boy hasn't contacted you is more to do with *his* own insecurity and cowardice.

IV) BEING "GIRLFRIEND AND BOYFRIEND"

What boys expect

If he does (miracle of miracles) get round to phoning you and arranging to meet up again, it looks like he's pretty keen on you. If it happens a few more times, you can quite safely start referring to this as a relationship – although not to his face! Boys are terrified of that sensation of the pair of you being joined at the hip, and although your new boyfriend may well be nuts about you, he probably won't want his life to change *too* radically. So don't go mentioning mortgages and how many kids you want, even in jest!

Now you may have very high expectations of this new romance, especially if it's your first, but it's important to realise that these may well clash with his.

At this early stage, boys tend to expect someone to have a laugh with and share lengthy goodnight kissing sessions. And not much more. This stage of getting to know each other and gradually getting closer is really exciting, so it'd be a shame to spoil it by constantly pondering how he feels, why he doesn't call every day and when he's going to tell you that he loves you – and forever questioning him about these things is one surefire way to annoy him, so be warned!

His Mates

We've already established that his mates and their approval are hugely important to your average lad, and it's important to bear this in mind when you start dating one. It could be that he's discovering a whole new emotional side to himself when he's alone with you, but it's highly unlikely that he'll want to share this *revelation* with his mates! He's also going to be very conscious of not giving them any reason to take the mick out of him now that he's got a girlfriend, so he'll very probably act differently with you when they're around.

He'll also want to carry on spending pretty much the same amount of time with them as he did before, so it's important not to put pressure on him to spend all his time with you. He'll really *resent* it if you try and stop him from going to football practice, rehearsing with his band or going on his usual lads' nights out.

Of course, if he insists on seeing his mates *all the time*, and rarely seems to have a spare evening for you, obviously that's not on. A lad whose mates are the be-all and end-all of his life will *not* make a great boyfriend.

Your Mates

It's quite probable that, however much he may like your closest female pals, he'll also be a bit scared of them. He may worry that, unlike him and his mates, you talk about *everything* with yours, dissecting each little detail of the relationship and slagging him off for everything he does wrong. This is a feeling that he will not enjoy.

It's important not to involve your friends – or indeed his – in the intricate workings of your relationship any more than necessary. Don't snigger with your mates and whisper about him when you see him approaching, or make him kiss you in front of them. Don't say things like, "Yeah, well Martine says you should blah blah," when you have a row. Your relationship is no one's business but *your own*, so don't let others involve themselves or judge him by what your friends think. You know yourself whether or not he makes you happy, so make up your own mind about him and his behaviour.

Of course, if he's completely rotten to you, then it might not do him any harm at all to be aware that your friends will have a word or two to say on the matter! But then, if he's completely rotten to you, you shouldn't be with him.

Meeting the Parents

If your new boyfriend fears the disapproval of your chums, it's nothing in comparison with his dread of encountering your parents. He knows that dads are traditionally suspicious of any chap who wants to dabble with their precious daughter, and that mums can be pretty hard-to-please when it comes to standards and suitability. Consequently, it's not a good idea to demand that he comes over for tea the minute you've started going out together.

If your boyfriend is older than you, or if your parents are particularly protective, they may well insist on meeting him and giving him a thorough checking out before letting you go ahead. If the choice is between enduring parental scrutiny or never seeing you again, hopefully he'll be keen enough to suffer for you and give a good impression! But at least do him the kindness of filling him in on any taboo subjects before he comes round, and helping the teatime conversation along as much as possible, so he doesn't end up squirming with embarrassment!

When he upsets you

Boys aren't too good at guessing that you're upset and they're *hopeless* at picking up subtle distress signals. They'll just put it down to moodiness when you're cross with them over something they've done (or *not* done) to make you unhappy, however obvious their crime may be to you. Bursting into tears confounds them even more, especially if it's just out of the blue. Most lads just don't think about feelings quite as much as you do, which means that the cause of your upset might be staring them in the face and stamping on their toe before they notice it.

So rather than put yourself – and him – through days of frustration and misunderstanding, the very best thing is just to tell him *straight*. He doesn't talk to you enough? Say so. Ignores you when his mates are around? He needs to be told. There's no point getting stroppy about it, nor showing him up in front of other people, because it'll only make things worse. Just find a quiet moment when the two of you are alone and feeling close, then gently tell him what's upsetting you. Then you can discuss it and, hopefully, sort things out between you.

20 things you should never make your boyfriend do...

- ✘ Kiss your teddies
- ✘ Ignore his exes
- ✘ Agree with you if you criticise his best mate
- ✘ Call you by a pet name if he doesn't want to
- ✘ Ring you every day
- ✘ Discuss his feelings for you in front of an audience
- ✘ Kiss you in front of your or his mates
- ✘ Give up football for you
- ✘ Write you love poems
- ✘ Radically alter his social life in order to spend time with you
- ✘ Tell you he loves you
- ✘ Admit that Take That/East 17/Johnny Depp, etc, are fanciable
- ✘ Pay for everything when you go out
- ✘ Radically change his appearance to please you
- ✘ Stop saying "fwoarr" when he sees pics of Pamela Anderson/Cindy Crawford/Michelle Pfeiffer, etc.
- ✘ Sit through slushy films if he can't stand them
- ✘ Stop him seeing his mates
- ✘ Insist that he become best pals with your mates
- ✘ Make him hold your hand in public
- ✘ Tell you all about his past love life in detail

WILL THIS RELATIONSHIP LAST?

At last! You've finally got it together with the boy you've been after for months, and you are officially "an item". Hurrah! But will it last? Or is it doomed to fail? Try our quiz and see...

1. On your first date, his main topic of conversation is...

a. *You.*

b. *Himself.*

c. *His ex-girlfriend.*

d. *The skill of Ryan Giggs.*

2. When he takes you home at the end of your first date, he...

a. *Stands awkwardly at your doorstep, and just sort of touches your arm when he says goodbye.*

b. *Gives you a little peck and says he'll see you soon.*

c. *Doesn't take you home? You have to brave the cold. night on your own.*

d. *Tries to remove several layers of your clothing on your front doorstep.*

3. Your parents are a bit concerned about this new guy in your life, and, insisting that they want to meet him, invite him over for tea. He...

a. *Refuses point-blank to meet them.*

b. *Wears his smartest shirt, combs his hair as neatly as possible and bravely grins his way through tea with the family.*

c. *Turns up in his usual garb, hardly utters a sound and plays footsie with you under the table.*

d. *Says okay, but not just yet.*

4. You've only been together a week when you have to stay home from school with a nasty bout of the flu'. He...

a. *Takes advantage of your absence and gets off with another girl.*

b. *Rings you every day to check you're okay.*

c. *Comes round but won't go past your threshold in case he gets infected, and laughingly tells you you look too awful to kiss anyway.*

d. *Comes round with flowers and a card and patiently plays games with you to cheer you up.*

5. You see him talking a bit too enthusiastically to another girl and you can't help but feel a bit jealous. When you ask who she is he ...

a. *Laughs at you and grins enigmatically every time you repeat the question.*

b. *Says, "None of your business".*

c. *Reassures you that she's an old friend who he hadn't seen in ages, and introduces you to her instantly.*

d. *Says, "Who? Oh, I dunno."*

QUIZQUIZQUIZ

6. When you're over your flu' for a special treat he ...

a. *Takes you to see your favourite band.*

b. *Takes you to see his favourite band*

c. *Takes you out somewhere. Anywhere!*

d. *Kisses you.*

7. You've just bought a somewhat daring outfit that you're rather proud of. When he arrives to take you out, he can't hide his horror. Does he say ...

a. *"You can't go out looking like that! Someone might see me with you!"*

b. *"Blimey, that's a bit loud. Still, if you like it, I do!"*

c. *"Erm... won't you be a bit cold?"*

d. *"There's something different about you. Er, hang on – no, don't help me, it's... you've had your hair cut!"*

8. You've just had your first row and both of you have walked off in a huff. Who's the first to try and patch things up?

a. *You are. But he tells you that he's sorry almost before you've opened your mouth.*

b. *He is.*

c. *Your best mate when she gets sick of seeing the pair of you snub each other all the time.*

d. *You are. And it takes quite a bit of persuading before he forgives you.*

9. You were meant to be going to a party together, when at the last minute your mum insists that you babysit for your little brother. Does he ...

a. *Go to the party without you.*

b. *Pop by to spend an hour with you before he goes to the party.*

c. *Stay in with you and brings his True Romance video along to cheer you both up.*

d. *Trie to persuade you to leave the little brat on his own as soon as your folks have gone, and come with him to the party as planned.*

10. You're having a bad hair day. Is his most likely comment ...

a. *"Oh, you always look good to me."*

b. *"You look a state, girl. Don't you have mirrors in your house?"*

c. *"Hah! You look just like Jim Carrey in Dumb And Dumber!"*

d. *"Oh, stop going on about your hair for God's sake."*

SCORES

1.	a. 15	b. 10	c. 0	d. 5
2.	a. 10	b. 15	c. 0	d. 5
3.	a. 0	b. 15	c. 5	d. 10
4.	a. 0	b. 10	c. 5	d. 15
5.	a. 5	b. 0	c. 15	d. 10
6.	a. 15	b.10	c. 5	d. 0
7.	a. 0	b. 15	d. 5	d. 10
8.	a. 10	b. 15	d. 5	d. 0
9.	a. 15	b. 10	c. 15	d. 5
10.	a. 15	b. 0	c. 5.	d. 10

115-150

This relationship's definitely built to last! Not only does he really like you, but he's also making most of the right moves to ensure that you want to stay with him. You have an awful lot in common and if you like him as much as he cares for you, you're on to a winner!

75-110

This one's most definitely got his heart in the right place, but he's not altogether in tune with what makes you or a relationship tick. He has a tendency to say the wrong thing and put his foot in it, so you'll need a bit of patience and guidance to get this one through the first few tricky weeks, but after that, hopefully it'll be true lurve.

45-70

Hmm, tricky this one. He does like you, but he's a bit too selfish to make any of the compromises you have to make in order to keep your loved one happy. He's expecting you to put up with a lot, so you're going to have to let him know in no uncertain terms that it's just not good enough!

0-40

This boy is just not good enough for you. He wants everything his way and seriously expects you to follow him around like an adoring puppy, ready to do whatever suits him. Do not put up with this shoddy behaviour.

V) BEING DUMPED/DUMPING

tell me WHY... Unsurprisingly, lads really hate being dumped. In fact, the fear of being chucked is one of the many things that stops lads from allowing themselves to fall in love. But one thing they hate still more is not being told *why* they're being given the elbow. It's really important that you're honest about your reasons, or his adoration could easily turn into anger and bitterness. If you've met someone else, you should tell him so. He'd much rather hear it from you than on the grapevine. If you think his mates are too important to him, you should say so too. He might disagree, but at least he'll know that this may cause problems with his future girlfriends. Or maybe you just feel that you're *incompatible*, and there's absolutely nothing wrong with telling him that either. It doesn't make either of you an awful person, it just means that you weren't well suited in the first place.

There's nothing worse than being told, "I don't want a relationship right now," or, "I just want to be friends," when you know that there's more to it than that, so show him you *respect* him and tell him the truth, kindly and gently. Being dishonest about your motives may make him angry and hateful and turn your ex into your enemy. Next thing you know, he's telling all the world what a cow you are and seeking his revenge!

Oh, you do IT Most lads are so horrified at the idea of being branded a heartless bastard, that they'd rather *you* ended the relationship, than have to do it themselves, just to let them off the hook. Forcing you, by one means or another, to chuck them makes them even more of a heartless bastard than if they'd merely done the chucking themselves, but most lads just can't face dealing with their emotions and being the chucker. They're far too wimpy for that.

They might start being a bit aloof and distant with you in the hope that you'll read between the lines and dump them. Or they might be relentlessly *rotten* until you lose your temper and tell them soundly to get lost. Or they might get off with other girls until you find out and refuse to continue your relationship with such a philandering two-timer. By any means necessary, it would seem, they'll put you off them sufficiently to tell them it's all over, thus relieving them of the guilt of having to hurt your feelings. The fact that they've hurt your feelings ten times more by messing you around seems to escape their notice!

WHEN HE DUMPS YOU

These are a few of the things boys say to try and soften the blow...

I just want to be friends

I don't want to hurt your feelings

I'm not good enough for you

You're wasting your time with me

I think we should just cool off for a while

I WANT TO SPREAD MY WINGS A BIT

You need to find someone worthy of you

YOU DESERVE BETTER THAN ME

If I stay with you I'll only hurt you

I can't trust myself to be there for you

I just need some space, man

I'm too irresponsible to have a girlfriend

I'm too young to settle down

PROBLEM PAGES

SHE THINKS I DON'T LIKE KISSING

I've been going out with Karen for six weeks now and I really like her. The only problem is, she thinks I don't like kissing. The fact is, I don't really know how to do it, and I don't want to disappoint her, so every time we kiss, I break away. What can I do?

Gavin, 13

Dear Gavin

If you don't want to hurt Karen's feelings and risk losing her, you're going to have to confide in her and quickly. It's very likely that Karen will end up thinking you don't actually like kissing her, and she'll soon get fed up with feeling rejected. The next time you're kissing, tell her you don't really have much kissing experience and ask her how she likes to be kissed. I'm sure she'll be more than happy to show you!

I'VE NEVER KISSED HER

I have a really embarrassing problem. I started going out with this girl about six weeks ago, and in all that time I've never kissed her. It's got so bad that her friends asked me if I want to finish with her. I really fancy her, but I'm afraid I'll make a prat of myself, especially now that there's so much pressure on me.

Andy, 14

Dear Andy,
It sounds to me like you're just suffering from first-kiss nerves. But really, there's nothing to be afraid of – and you'll soon be wondering what took you so long! The next time you're alone with your girlfriend, just put your arms round her and gently pull her to you. Then shut your eyes and put your lips on hers. There's no secret technique that no one's told you about, it really is just something that comes naturally once you get started. Practise on the back of your hand, if need be, and observe how people kiss in films if you want a little extra guidance, but really, there's nothing to it. Good luck!

I SAID I'D PHONE

I asked this girl out and we went to the pictures together. Afterwards I said I'd phone her, but I got cold feet, and when I bumped into her a week later I went and acted like nothing had happened. Is it too late to phone her now? I still really like her.

Jeremy, 15

Dear Jeremy,

If you really like this girl, you have to let her know at once. She'll be feeling hurt and rejected, so it's up to you to reassure her that you do want to see her again. It's awkward, of course, if you let your nerves get the better of you when you saw her, but she deserves an explanation. Ring her up, apologise for not getting in touch and say you'd like to see her so you can explain. She may say okay, or she may tell you to get lost, but either way you'll be kicking yourself for months if you don't try to rectify the situation. Now get to it!

The conclusion on boys

So there you have it. Boys aren't aliens at all, but they *do* tend to have different ways of looking at things than girls, and that can lead to huge amounts of confusion when they have to deal with each other. This confusion is really based on mutual misunderstanding. You now know that boys are just as insecure, sensitive and keen to get close to someone as girls are.

Just because boys are less open with their feelings than girls, it doesn't mean they don't have them. With a bit of work, patience and care, you'll find that some lads can make excellent friends and boyfriends – and they're definitely worth the effort. But then, of course, if you happen to meet one with two heads and green tentacles, steer well clear!

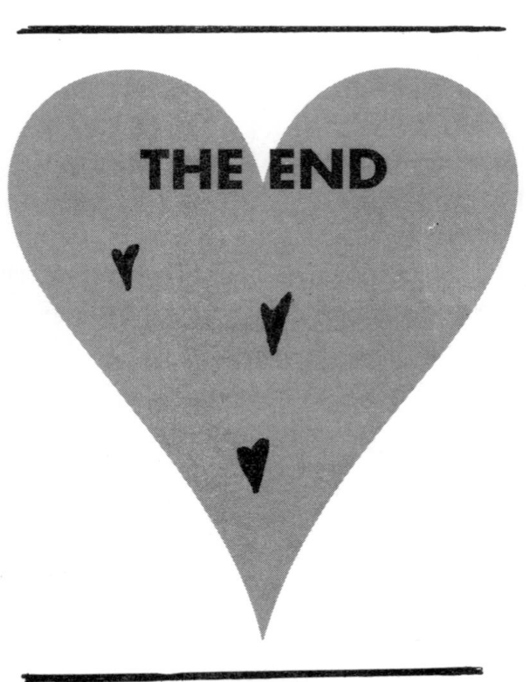
THE END

OTHER TEENAGE BOOKS

PUBLISHED BY

piccadilly press

DON'T BLAME ME – I'M A GEMINI:

Astrology for Teenagers

by Reina James-Reinstein and Mike Reinstein

"...ideal...Reina Reinstein writes knowledgeably in an entertaining way"

SCHOOL LIBRARIAN

FOR WEDDINGS, A FUNERAL AND WHEN YOU CAN'T FLUSH THE LOO

by Jane Goldman

"Jolly sensible and friendly"

THE INDEPENDENT

"Jane Goldman's tips and tactics guide is perceptive"

THE TIMES

GET BETTER GRADES

Cool Study Skills for Red Hot Results

by Margie Agnew, Steve Barlow,
Lee Pascal and Steve Skidmore

"Teenager friendly and witty...amusing advice"

THE INDEPENDENT

JUST DON'T MAKE A SCENE, MUM

The Trials and Tribulations of 5 Teenagers

by Rosie Rushton

"An essential read ... Belly-achingly funny"

19 MAGAZINE

"Cool and diverting comedy"

THE TIMES

YOU'RE MY BEST FRIEND – I HATE YOU

FRIENDS – GETTING, LOSING AND KEEPING THEM

by Rosie Rushton

"Lots of humorous and sensible advice"

OBSERVER